T0106285

Conscious Parent, Conscious Child

Conscious Parent, Conscious Child

Raising a Happy Confident Child Without Fear

CAMILLE BROWNING

Photographs by Bethanne Staton

BALBOA
PRESS
A DIVISION OF HAY HOUSE

Photographs by Bethanne Staton.

Balboa Press books may be ordered through booksellers or by contacting:

Balboa Press
A Division of Hay House
1663 Liberty Drive
Bloomington, IN 47403
www.balboapress.com
1-(877) 407-4847

ISBN: 978-1-4525-4318-5 (sc)
ISBN: 978-1-4525-4319-2 (hc)
ISBN: 978-1-4525-4317-8 (e)

Library of Congress Control Number: 2011961415

Printed in the United States of America

Balboa Press rev. date: 12/16/2011

DEDICATION

With deep gratitude and love, I dedicate this book
to five of my greatest teachers—my children:
Bethanne, LeAnne, Jonathan, Benjamin, and Samuel.

Acknowledgements

To all of you who have made this book possible, I give to you my heart felt appreciation.

My husband, Danny, you not only believed in me and encouraged me to write this book, but you insisted that I speak the truth as I see it, regardless of any perceived criticism I could receive. Thank you for your patience with me and always allowing me to change and grow.

My children and friends who helped with the initial editing, listening to my ideas, and giving me helpful input, you confirmed for me that what I have to say has merit and is worth the effort to put it into a book.

Dallas, Brooklyn, and Rockman, you give me a chance to experience the joy of being your Mee Mee. You have caused me to see life differently.

Sandi Dietrich, my Rapid Eye technician and friend, without you I do not think I would have ever stepped out of my fears enough to write this book. Thank you for helping me see who I really am. It has been quite a journey.

Jean Miller, thank you for your friendship and assistance in helping me see my purpose, speak my truth and live from my heart.

Ranae Johnson, founder of Rapid Eye Technology and the Skills for Life program, thank you for your vision and bringing it into creation.

Lisa Booher, what a great job of editing, even with the demands of parenting four small children.

Janice Starling, your help and suggestions inspired the artwork. Thank you for your right-brain assistance.

And to all of my Rapid Eye clients, thank you for the privilege of walking with you on your journey. As we worked together, I saw the light within you and I am truly honored to know you.

TABLE OF CONTENTS

INTRODUCTION

If you are reading this book, I believe that you were lead by the Divine to do so because there is something for you within these pages. My intention in creating this work is to touch, move and inspire you in a way that will change your life, the lives of your children, and the lives of everyone who crosses your path. This book is for those of you who have children, those who are planning to have children, and those who work with children. It is my desire also that grandparents be inspired and find ways to increase the positive influence they have on their precious grandchildren. Perhaps you feel you are doing a poor job and do not know what to do differently. Maybe you feel you are doing a pretty good job but feel that something is missing and you would like to do better. I believe we live in perilous yet wondrous times. The power is in us to make a difference, to do things differently, to BE a different way.

I am the mother of five children. They are now grown, some with children of their own. I can honestly say that I did the very best that I knew how and I have no regrets. Would I do things differently if I had it to do over? Many things, yes. Why? Because I now know better. "We do the best we can with what we know, and *"when we know better, we do better"* (Dr. Maya Angelou). This is how we grow and evolve. We come to this planet to learn, to get experience, to become conscious, to create joy. Raising children is what taught me much of what I now am. You might say that my children raised me! By the time I became more conscious and learned how to be a parent, my children were grown.

So it is too late for me, or is it? I still have a relationship with them. It is now an adult-to-adult relationship, but I can BE different now. I cannot be the mother of young children again, nor do I want to be. But I can BE the conscious person I have become, and I can change the energy of the new adult relationships. I can also experience my grandchildren in a different way. Is it not wonderful to get a second chance? Not only to change the energy of my relationships with my adult children but to BE a different way with my grandchildren.

The message of this book is one of hope, of new possibilities, of looking at things in a new way. It is also a message of forgiveness and acceptance. We are our own worst critic. It is time to let go of guilt and stop beating up ourselves. It is time to wake up and do differently those things that are not working for us and our children.

My desire is to open the door for you to awaken as you put all your old notions aside and consider some new ones. As you finish the last page, please consider all the new notions along with the old and take those that work for you. The Divine in you will let you know the truth of how best to BE a more conscious human being and a more conscious parent, and how to assist children to BE conscious, happy, confident, and to BE the change needed in our world.

The examples and stories in this book are real experiences. Many of them come from my private Rapid Eye Technology practice. In some cases the names or minor details have been changed to protect their identity. I am grateful to the many clients with whom I have done sessions, and I am honored to have been part of their journey. I have benefited greatly from knowing them. As I have looked into their eyes, I have seen that we are all more alike than different. I have always looked for the divine light in each of them; it was *always* there.

During the many hours of writing this book, I realized the great benefit this project has been to me. You might say *I am learning my book.* Great advice was given to me during my youth. It was this: "Seek out of the best books, words of wisdom." I have come to believe that we all have words of wisdom to share with others. Perhaps everyone has a book in them to share with the world. Go to any book store, and it is almost overwhelming the number of books that are available. I believe that everyone has things of value to share with others: things that will touch, move, or inspire someone that no one else can. Again, it is my intention that this book fall into the hands of those who are seeking that which is within these pages. I am honored to be a part of your journey toward living a more conscious life and toward helping your child to be the same. Namaste`

Section I
MAKING CHANGES IN YOU

For God hath not given us the spirit of fear; but of power,
and of love, and of a sound mind. (Holy Bible)

CHAPTER 1
Today's Paradigm of Fear
Changing It to Love

I was twenty-eight years old when I had my first child. I remember how excited but also how scared I was. Being a mom was what I had looked forward to since I was a child. It is what I always wanted to do. I had other dreams and hopes for myself, but marrying a good man, living in a big house, and raising a family was somehow prominent in my mind from an early age.

I did all the right things. I graduated from college, worked for a while, married a good man, got pregnant, gave up my job, and proceeded to read everything I could find about how to have the perfect pregnancy and birth, and how to be the perfect mom. Needless to say I would then have perfect children. After all, was that not my job, to see that my children had everything they needed to become, well, perfect?

I was not completely delusional. I knew I was not perfect. As I look back, I realize how inadequate I really felt. I suppose that is some of the reason I read everything I could find on pregnancy,

3

birth, and parenting. I took it all to heart. I gave it my best shot. *I did the very best I knew how.*

I took it on as my job to not only teach my children everything they needed to do to be perfect human beings, but to protect them from the big bad world. I wanted them to avoid all the dangers out there. I started out by teaching them the dangers of getting run over by a car if they got in the street. "If you get in the street without looking, you'll get run over by a car." Then it went to food, drugs, and sex. "Junk food makes you sick and unhealthy. Drugs will ruin your life and kill you. If you don't learn to read and get a good education you won't be able to support yourself. Premarital sex causes disease and unhappiness. Marry the wrong person and you will be miserable the rest of your life." Was I not just teaching them the consequences of their actions? Was I not just protecting them from the bad things in the world?

Protecting them was another big responsibility I took on. I was hyper-vigilant. I vowed to be the mom who was always there. They would always be fed the best food. They would always be in my sight, so nothing *bad* would happen to them. Even though I perceived the world as a dangerous place, I had high hopes for my children. I just knew I could mold them into what I thought they should be.

Today, thirty-four years later, my children are grown, I have grandchildren, and I still have a very good man who has been by my side all these years, patiently watching my metamorphosis. Looking back, I see that my world view during those early years was one of fear. For the most part, our society is still one of fear. When we parent from a paradigm of fear, we instill fear into our children. The thing on which we put our focus, we attract to us, and we get that which we fear. Fear is the opposite of love. If the focus is on fear, love is pushed aside.

Did I love my children? Yes! I had the very best intentions in my parenting. I hope they know that they were loved. It is my hope, also, that they know that I did the very best I knew how.

I no longer beat myself up for my parenting choices. I have come too far in my own personal work to do that anymore, nor do I wallow in blame or guilt for not knowing any better at the time. In actuality, I did many things that absolutely assisted them in being happy productive adults today. Many things I would not change. However, I now look at my parenting from a new perspective. Remember again the words spoken by Dr. Angelou, "When you know better, you do better." Even though I cannot go back and *do it better*, this book is an attempt to help *you* do better, no matter where you are on your parenting journey. Taking a good look at ourselves with the intention to really see ourselves, not with judgement, but with awakened eyes, is a step toward conscious, joyful living. The intention of this book is to help you assist your child to live a conscious, joyful life. **Because you cannot teach what you do not live, you must *live* consciously yourself to teach that to your child.**

Fear

Fear is defined as an unpleasant emotion caused by the belief that someone or something is dangerous, likely to cause pain, or a threat. Also, it is a feeling of anxiety concerning the outcome of something and the likelihood of something unwelcome happening, a feeling of disquiet or apprehension and uneasiness. Synonyms of fear: terror, fright, horror, panic, agitation, trepidation, dread, dismay, anxiety, worry, unease, nervousness, and foreboding. I feel my energy level going down just writing these fear words.

Negative words and emotions cause unhappiness, and even physical dis-ease.

I spent much of my childhood and adult life filled with fear. I was afraid of not being good enough or not smart enough. I was afraid my parents would not love me if I was not perfect. I was afraid I would make a mistake and go to hell and afraid God would be upset with me and not want me in heaven. I refrained from doing many things that I would have liked to do because I was afraid of what people would say, and I was afraid I would fail. I wanted to be a teacher, but I was afraid to take the classes in college that required me to get up in front of my peers. I was afraid that I would be tempted to have sex before I was married, so I did not date much. I was afraid my parents would not love me, so I did everything to please them. I was afraid of God, so I tried my very best to live all of what I thought were his commandments.

Many would say fear kept me out of a lot of trouble. Yes, it did. I am grateful that I avoided many of the pitfalls that I would probably still be living with had I taken a different path: addictions, sexual disease, teen pregnancy, and early marriage, to name a few. But I believe I did many good things for the wrong reasons. I believe a child can grow up and make good choices out of *love* instead of fear. Anyone who makes choices out of fear misses out on life. You cannot experience fear and love at the same time. They do not exist together.

Many people, especially in the Christian community, have the belief that we should *fear God*. It does say that in the Bible. Yet, also in the Bible, I John 4:18, it says, "There is no fear in love; but perfect love casteth out fear: because fear hath torment. He that feareth is not made perfect in love." Repeatedly in the Bible it is said that *GOD IS LOVE*. This says to me that fear and love cannot abide together. Many spiritual teachers today also teach that fear and love are exact opposites. Here are a few:

- "Fear and love can never be experienced at the same time. It is always our choice as to which of these emotions we want . . . Love, then, is letting go of fear." (Gerald Jampolsky, *Love is Letting Go of Fear*)
- "Essentially there are two overriding emotions—love and fear. And those two emotional states cannot be experienced simultaneously . . . You cannot have God and have fear too. Every fear represents a disbelief in God at that moment. Keep uppermost in mind these two observations. One from the scriptures, 'I will fear no evil, for thou art with me.'" (Wayne W. Dyer, *There's a Spiritual Solution to Every Problem*)
- "Love is what we were born with. Fear is what we have learned here." (Marianne Williamson, *A Return to Love*)

My favorite teaching from the New Testament is II Timothy 1:7. "For God hath not given us the spirit of fear; but of power, and of love, and of a sound mind." This has become my mantra. I have it printed and posted on a wall in my home. It is my reminder to let go of my fears and to embrace love and real power which comes from God.

Many things in our society, indeed on our planet, illustrate how much fear rules our world. We have war because we fear we will lose our freedoms. We fear that we will be left powerless. We fear societies and nations who have beliefs other than ours. Jesus, as well as other great masters, taught love, not hate and fear. He taught peace, not war. Statements attributed to Jesus, such as "love one another" and "love your enemy," are throughout the New Testament and other works accredited to his teachings.

Look at the political arena. Most politicians do not talk much about anything positive. They spend much of their time pointing their finger and telling us why we should be afraid of what will happen if we vote for their opponent.

Our schools, for the most part, use fear to teach. Children are afraid to move out of their seats, afraid to speak, afraid to think for themselves, afraid of giving the wrong answer, afraid of making bad grades and failing, afraid of being scolded, corrected, criticized. There is even fear of death from guns. Have we become so afraid of everything that we have created a vicious cycle of fear creating fear? Have we become so focused on the violence, ignorance, and misbehavior, that we attract more violence, ignorance, and misbehavior?

Many parents have opted to home school. Home school can be an opportunity to teach from a basis of love. This can be a wonderful option. Sadly, many parents take their children out of public school out of fear, only to continue the fear-based thinking at home.

Drug addiction is another thing that we fear. We have even declared war on it! It is the same with many of the health issues of our day. Instead of a war on cancer, what would happen if we declared love on it?

Religion and church attendance can provide a community of brotherhood, friendship, social activities, and a means of service to others. It can also be a means of moral guidance, self betterment, and spiritual growth. Most religions talk of love. However, fear is often used in an effort to keep us safe and on a path of morality and goodness. Think back on the dictionary definition of fear: anxiety, apprehension, terror, fright, panic, worry, uneasiness, nervousness. God is not these things, but these things have crept into our churches. As fear creeps in, I believe that love creeps out. If God is love, does God creep out, too? However well intentioned a church is, fear-based religion creates more problems than it solves.

Love

We have identified fear and considered what it creates in our lives, but let us not focus on fear. Let us turn our attention and focus toward what we really want more of: LOVE. Remember: we get more of that on which we focus.

There is the Native American story of two wolves. The grandfather told his grandson, "The battle is between two wolves inside of us all. One is FEAR. The other is LOVE." The grandson thought for a minute and then asked, "Which wolf wins?" The grandfather replied, "The one you feed."

"Eventually you will come to understand that **love heals everything**, and **love is all there is**." (Gary Zukav, *The Seat of the Soul*.)

Nelson Mandela quoted the following in his inaugural speech in 1994. It is one of the most inspiring statements of our day. It is from the book *A Return to Love* by Marianne Williamson.

Our deepest fear is not that we are inadequate.
Our deepest fear is that we are powerful beyond measure.
It is our light, not our darkness, that most frightens us.
We ask ourselves,
who am I to be brilliant, gorgeous, talented, and fabulous?
Actually, who are you not to be?
You are a child of God.

Your playing small doesn't serve the world.
There's nothing enlightened about shrinking
so that other people won't feel insecure around you.
We are all meant to shine, as children do.
We are born to make manifest the glory of God
that is within us.
It's not just in some of us,
it's in everyone.
And as we let our own light shine,
we unconsciously give other people
permission to do the same.
As we are liberated from our own fear,
our presence automatically liberates others.

Is it possible to change the paradigm of fear to one of love? Is it possible to liberate ourselves from our fear? I believe that it is. Just imagine individuals, families, schools, churches, communities, governments, and nations operating from a paradigm of love. We can let go of fear and embrace love. When we let go of fear, what is left is love. Love is who we are. Love is all there is.

There are those in our educational communities who are living their lives from love and making a difference in their world. Montessori schools, which have sprung up around the country, seem to have let go of fear and figured out how to teach from a place of love. Their methods are used in private and public schools throughout the world. Marie Montessori wanted to make the world a better place by helping children to not only have more meaningful lives as children, but to help them contribute to humanity itself.

Another interesting approach to education is seen in a private school in Fairhope, Alabama, near Mobile. It is called The School of Organic Education and was founded in 1907. The premise of their methods is based on honoring and treating all children with respect and dignity. The first of three fundamental requisites for their teachers is that they love, understand, and are sincerely interested in children.

Look around you for examples of love in action. There are those in our schools, churches, and communities who operate from love instead of fear. The more you look, the more you will see.

Children See Love
Because They ARE Love

A group of four to eight-year-old children were asked, "What does love mean?" The following are some of their answers:

- "When my grandmother got arthritis, she couldn't bend over and paint her toenails anymore. So my grandfather does it for her all the time, even when his hands got arthritis too. That's love."

- "When someone loves you, the way they say your name is different. You just know that your name is safe in their mouth."

- "Love is when my mommy makes coffee for my daddy and she takes a sip before giving it to him, to make sure the taste is OK."

- "Love is when you tell a guy you like his shirt, then he wears it every day."

- "During my piano recital, I was on a stage and I was scared. I looked at all the people watching me and saw my daddy waving and smiling. He was the only one doing that. I wasn't scared anymore."

- "My mommy loves me more than anybody. You don't see anyone else kissing me to sleep at night."

- "Love is when Mommy gives Daddy the best piece of chicken."

- "Love is when Mommy sees Daddy smelly and sweaty and still says he is handsomer than Robert Redford."

- "Love is when your puppy licks your face even after you left him alone all day."

- "Love is when Mommy sees Daddy on the toilet and she doesn't think it's gross."

Leo Buscaglia once talked about a contest he was asked to judge to find the most caring child. The winner was a four-year-old child whose next door neighbor was an elderly gentleman who had recently lost his wife. Upon seeing the man cry, the little boy went into the old gentleman's yard, climbed onto his lap, and just sat there. When his mother asked what he had said to the neighbor, the little boy said, "Nothing. I just helped him cry."

Love *is* what these children were born with. They *see* love because they *are* love. Look deeply at your child. Look deeply at yourself. Love is there. When you see it and feel it, you begin to realize that LOVE really is ALL THERE IS. It is who we are.

Exercises
For Creating New Parenting Patterns

At the end of each chapter will be exercises to help you create a new and better way to live the principles of conscious parenting. We must take steps to do things in a different way so that we can change our old patterns and old ways of doing things. I suggest journaling as a way to help you understand yourself and your journey with your child. Writing down your efforts will give you an increased understanding and a record of how you are doing for your reference.

1. List some of the fears you had as a child. Do you still have these or similar fears?

2. List ways you are currently parenting from your fears?

3. From the list in question 2 above, how can you change these fears to love?

4. Make a list of the love you see in your community, your child, and yourself.

5. Have a conversation with your child on what you have learned from chapter 1. Commit to them how you plan to be, with these new understandings.

Children are so in the present moment in everything they do.

CHAPTER 2
Becoming Conscious

C onsciousness is defined as the state of being awake and aware; aware of yourself and your situation. Unconscious is defined as unmindful of, oblivious to, insensible to, indifferent to, unaware of, unknowing of. Many people, although physically awake, are spiritually asleep and unaware. I believe that we must be awake and aware of who we are before we can be aware of who our children are. *We* must be conscious to help our children be conscious.

There are four stages of consciousness:

1. You don't know that you don't know.
2. You know that you don't know.
3. You don't know that you know.
4. You know that you know.

You are probably not in the first stage, or you would not be reading this book. If you have a desire to know, you are probably in the second stage. As you awaken you move through these stages toward *knowing that you know*. This is total awareness. I know of no one who is in this stage *all* the time, although I am sure there are enlightened beings out there who are at this level. The goal is to become conscious and to know that you know. To be on the path of consciousness is to awaken a little more every day. Get to know yourself and awaken to your Divine self.

Knowing Yourself

So who are we? We are first and foremost, spirit beings. Our spirit (the real us) is housed in a physical body. It has been said that we are not human beings having aspiritual experience, but rather we are spiritual beings having a human experience. We did not begin our journey at birth. Birth is only the beginning of our human experience. Different belief systems have different notions about how and where we began, but most agree that we exist beyond our physical bodies, that we existed before this earth life and will exist after this life.

Our spirit body enters our physical body at birth. Our spirit is light. The illusion is that we left the light and are always looking outside ourselves for light and truth. Reality is that we came to this earth with that light, and it exists in every cell of our bodies. The illusion is that we left God and that we are separate from Him. Reality is that we are still connected with the Source of all light. We ARE the light. We need not look outside of ourselves for light and truth and for the answers to our life problems, but look within to find light, truth, God, and all the answers for our life. IT IS IN US!

Loving Yourself

We come into the world as a baby innately knowing that we are completely lovable. Our experiences most often convince us otherwise. Then our whole life is spent trying to regain that original innate knowing of who we are. Instead of asking a child "What do you want to be when you grow up?" why not instill a sense of "I love who you are, just the way you are. You don't have to BE anything other than who you are right now. You are loved. You are lovable." When our child knows this, nothing else matters, and they are free to live life to the fullest; but before you can instill this in your child, you must return to the belief that *you* are loved and lovable.

Judging

"We do not judge the people we love." (Jean-Paul Sartre) Who is the one person we judge more than any other? Ourselves. As we come to love ourselves, we are able to put aside our self judgements. Even our judgements of others are only a reflection of what we think and feel about ourselves. (More about mirrors in chapter 6) Getting to know yourself can be painful if you do not love yourself. We can be the cruelest to our own selves. How do we look at ourselves and our perceived flaws and mistakes with love and understanding instead of judgement and contempt? My friends and I have a thing we say that helps us remember to set our judgements aside and to just look at our behavior without the judgement. We say, "I am noticing . . ." By just noticing a behavior, we can detach from the behavior and just look at it. Look with love and compassion at yourself as you would with a small child learning to walk. We are children learning. Getting to know yourself in your journey to awareness and consciousness is not about beating up on yourself. It is about accepting and loving yourself as you are, without the judgements.

Being Present and in the Moment

Paul McKenna has put together a weight-loss program that includes what he calls *eating consciously.* He recommends eating with total focus on each bite of food you put in your mouth. "Enjoy every bite," he tells us. In today's fast-paced world, we gobble our food so quickly that we sometimes cannot remember what we ate or how much we ate! Consequently we eat more than we should. He says food should be eaten slowly and consciously so we eat less and enjoy it more. Deepak Chopra also advocates conscious eating. To change our pattern of eating too much and too fast to a new pattern of eating consciously takes effort. It is said that it takes twenty-one consecutive days to change a habit and create a new pattern and a new neural pathway. At first our attempt to change feels awkward and difficult, but if we stay with it, it can become as easy as the old pattern.

Being conscious, present, and in the moment with food can bring great rewards to our physical body. Being present and in the moment with our children can also bring great rewards. If you become present with your children, you enjoy them more, they feel loved and lovable, they become less needy and demanding, and they will be happy and confident. Children are the teachers here. They are so in the moment in every thing they do. Time stands still for them (much to our frustration at times).

When my daughter was about two years old we went on a family walk. She smelled every flower she saw, which was quite a few. A family walk with little ones can be pleasant if we stay present, or it can be unpleasant if our focus is on "Hurry, hurry! Keep up with us. Don't do that. Don't touch." and thinking "Let's just get through this without a fiasco." Smelling flowers was brand new to her, and she was enjoying every one of them.

She was conscious. She was present and in the moment. She was experiencing joy. Is that not what we all want? Joy? Follow a child's lead and learn how to do it. They have it, until we take it away from them by not allowing them to be present and by not being present with them.

I have observed that when a child brings a picture they have drawn, a rock they have found, or has something to tell a significant adult in their life, that if the adult does not respond or they half-heartedly respond, this child is very likely to come back over and over again to the point of irritation to the adult, or they will misbehave in a way that triggers the adult to misbehave toward the child. However, when the adult stops and becomes present by turning their full attention to the child, the child is happy and quickly goes back to their own play. The number of times the child returns for attention is much less than the child whose parent is not present with them. My conclusion after years of observing the interaction of children and adults is that the more attention the adult gives (the more present and in the moment), the less clingy, needy, and disruptive the child is.

Recently I was driving alone in my car. As I looked to the left I saw a yard of green winter grass. On the grass were hundreds of black birds. It was a beautiful sight. As I slowly drove by, the movement of my car caused the birds to begin to fly. It was like a wave as the birds closest to the car began to fly up and to the left. The other birds followed, and then they reversed their flight pattern as they flew directly over me and my car. It was a moment in which I was present. It was as if time stood still, and I felt one with the birds. The birds and I were created by the same divine presence and for that moment I felt one with them and the divine presence. That feeling of joy and oneness is the gift which comes from being present and in the moment.

It is vital to be present with your child. Being present with them means enjoying the child the same way I enjoyed the birds. It is letting time stand still for a moment and feeling the joy and gift of the child. It is feeling one with them and sensing the divine presence in both of you.

Being present with your child involves not wanting something from them. "Clean your room. Do your homework. Eat your vegetables. Do this. Don't do that." Being present requires that when you are with your child that you *touch, listen to, look at, and even speak to* your child with such focus, awareness, and awe that you *feel* the gift of the moment in such a way that you are not parent and child, but rather two divine beings experiencing life together.

I was having lunch with my two-and-a-half-year-old grandson. He was very fascinated by the milk in his glass. He put his hand in the glass and was enjoying the feel of the milk. He was present, but his tender feelings were hurt when I said, "Oh, don't put your hand in your milk." He withdrew his hand, and his lower lip quivered. I had unthinkingly shattered his feeling of oneness with the milk. I quickly put my hand in his milk and said, "Oh, let's *do* put our hands in the milk and see how that feels!" Our relationship was restored, and we became one as I enjoyed the divine in this glorious little boy who was experiencing how milk feels. His experience, had I not restored it, would have been one of separation, guilt, and *fear*.

The gift you receive for being awake, aware, and conscious is feeling one with the Divine. You will also feel alive and joyful. The outcome of being spiritually asleep and unaware is feeling separate from God, your child, and others. You will also feel lifeless, dull, and bored. Once you get a taste of the fruit of "awakeness," you will want more.

Parenting in the Present

Most of us, because we live in the past, also parent from the past. We parent from our childhood. If we had a traumatic or negative experience as a child (and we all did), we may parent from the perspective of our child self. If this is the case, we have a child parenting a child. As we become more conscious and awake, we can parent from the present moment, as an adult.

A young mother perceived her own parents as being too regimented and strict when it came to meals and bed time. She took the opposite approach with her own children, letting them go to bed whenever they wanted and eat whatever they wanted. She knew that having a little more order would benefit them all, but felt rebellious whenever she thought about it. Instead of doing what she felt worked best for her and her children, she did the opposite and allowed a rebellious child (her past self) to make the choices for her children's meal and bed times. When she realized what she was doing, she stepped into her adult self and made choices that were somewhere between the rigidness of her own childhood and the chaos that her children were experiencing. The children did well with the new "adult" parent. The children were happy and mom was happy.

Without realizing it, we have expectations of our children, usually based on our own upbringing. Two women from different backgrounds have totally different expectations based on how they were raised. In Sue's family, both of her parents had attended college. When she and her siblings were of age, they attended college. Her parents never insisted they get an education past high school. It just seemed to happen. The mostly unspoken expectation was *when you graduate from high school, you go to college.* In Mary's home, on the other hand, no one had gone to college. When she and her siblings graduated from high school, they got a job. There were no expectations of college, and they never considered it an option. Mary has not "awoken" to the possibility that advanced education could benefit her or her children. She is living her life unconsciously and walking through life asleep and unaware of anything other than how she was raised. This is parenting from the unconscious expectations founded in her past.

A mother of several girls was molested as an eight-year-old child. She lived in constant fear that her daughters would be molested also. She was extremely overprotective and lived in the constant state of fear that her children would suffer as she had. At times she even took on the persona of an extremely frightened eight-year-old child. It was as though a frightened, paranoid, eight-year-old child was parenting her children.

My father used to always ask, when we did something that did not work for us, "Well, did you learn anything?" It is a great question to ask. Looking at our past and learning from it can be of value. For the awakened soul, we must look and learn. We have also learned many positive things from our family of origin that we want to *consciously* bring with us. We need only eliminate the things that do not work. Do not throw out everything . . . only that which does not work. Even if you come from an extremely dysfunctional family, there are always good things to bring with you to parent your own children.

Parenting in the past is doing things the way we were raised and not considering any other way. It is also parenting from the place of our wounded inner-child. Parenting in the present is considering the ways of our past, but also considering other possibilities. It is parenting not from the wounded inner-child, but from the healed adult. Who is parenting your child? Hopefully it is a mature, conscious, awake, and aware adult.

Exercises
For Creating New Parenting Patterns

1. Each morning look at yourself in the mirror (look in your eyes) and say out loud, "I love you just the way you are. You are loved and lovable."

2. Each time you catch yourself seeing a perceived mistake or error in your child, just notice it without judgement and imagine your child when he or she was learning to walk. Journal your experiences in doing this.

3. Practice being present with your child and journal your experiences.

4. What ways are you parenting from your childhood?

*Reclaim your power to receive constant personal guidance
from the Divine. We are more powerful than we realize.*

CHAPTER 3
Finding Answers

I have always believed that if I look for an answer, I will find it. The Buddhist proverb "When the student is ready, the teacher will appear" is very apt. If you are not ready, the teacher will not appear, because even if it did, you would not see it.

Looking for Answers

In 2001, I was at a place in my life that I felt *what else is there?* I thought I was happy. I had a good marriage and children, and we were okay financially. I had my share of ups and downs, but overall, I was doing all right. I was not exactly sure what I was feeling, but somehow I knew there was something more.

It was during this time also, that one of my daughters was depressed. As a result she was failing college. She could not sleep most of the time, but when she did, she had nightmares. She struggled to make herself go to class only to get there and have a panic attack and have to leave. I dreaded to hear the phone ring. She called almost every day because she felt so bad. I did not know what to do for her except listen. We looked everywhere for answers: doctors, nutrition, books, school counselors, church counselors, psychologists. When we thought there was nowhere else to turn, she read a book by Carol Tuttle, *Remembering Wholeness*. Carol tells her story of depression and how she overcame it. She talked about a technique called Rapid Eye Technology.

My daughter was excited as she read the book and learned more about this therapy. She found a technician five hours away. She said, "Mom, we have tried all the other therapies, and none of it has worked very well. I would like to try this."

I could see an excitement in her that could not be ignored. What I found on the internet seemed a bit weird, but we had looked for so long to no avail. I felt like I was at the end of my rope. So I let go of the rope and agreed to travel five hours with her to try out this strange technique with someone about whom we knew nothing. Even though I was apprehensive, deep inside I knew we had found an answer. It was a big leap of faith, but we stepped into it.

My daughter did a series of sessions. I committed to do one just to see what it was and to make sure she was not getting into something . . . of the devil. (I cannot believe I had so much fear about that!) After I did a session, I wanted to do more. We ended up doing four sessions each. I felt better and happier than I had my whole life. After we returned home, my daughter's nightmares stopped completely. She was able to sleep. The panic attacks stopped, and the depression was much better.

This experience was so profound for me that I took the training to become a Rapid Eye Technician. It changed our lives, and I see it change the lives of my clients. Rapid Eye Technology is the best tool I know of to get to know yourself, to know the real you, the you that is hidden beneath years of negative emotions caused by the traumas in your life that you may not even realize or remember.

Rapid Eye Technology

Rapid Eye Technology (RET) is a natural energy healing therapy that releases stress and trapped negative emotional energy from the body, incurred from wounds from the past, helping one to move forward in life with a sense of well-being, peace, and joy. RET assists healing on all levels (physical, emotional, and mental), and we then awaken to our spiritual selves and can then create our life from this spiritual place. Using blinking, breathing, and eye movement techniques, RET simulates a condition of sleep known as Rapid Eye Movement (REM). REM is our body's natural emotional release mechanism. During REM sleep we process, clear, and integrate our day's experiences. RET simulates REM sleep by moving an eye-directing device quickly in front of the client's eyes in the neurolinguistic patterns of REM sleep. The client is totally awake and aware during this process. As the client blinks and breathes deeply, the trapped messages and negative energy are accessed and released from the body. The client is then free to see their life from the spiritual perspective, and move out of the past and live in the present.

For more information about RET go to www. rapideyetechnology.com or read Dr. Ranae Johnson's book, *Reclaim Your Light Through the Miracle of RAPID EYE TECHNOLOGY.*

Books

There are many good books to start you on a path of knowing yourself. There is a list in the back of this book of many that have helped me. Read what you feel drawn to. When my sister will go in a book store, often a book will just jump out at her, or her eyes will suddenly fall on a book. She says it is always exactly what she needs at that time. It does not happen like that for me. I will hear of a book, and it may pique my interest. I will check it out, and some will stir something in me. When I feel that stirring within, I read the book. I am always open to new learning and new ways of looking at things. Books can be a means to assist you on your journey to know yourself and become more conscious.

Meditation & Prayer

Meditation and prayer is another must in awakening to the divine within. Whether you believe in God or not, taking personal time to sit quietly and silence your mind is of great benefit. We live in such a noisy, fast-paced world. Many people keep a radio, television, or music on all the time. It is my notion that this is done because of an unconscious fear of being alone. It is an avoidance of getting to know the divine and of getting to know yourself. Getting to know the real you can be profound and spiritually healing. It can create a more peaceful and joyful life. The Bible says, "Be still and know that I am God." This is meditation. Every religion or belief system, whether Eastern or Western, practices some sort of prayer and/or mediation.

I have experienced a change in my own prayers over the years. I used to do all the talking and not much listening, telling God how bad things were and asking Him to change it. I would beg Him to change other people's behavior that I judged as bad or wrong. I would try to control my children even in my prayers by telling God to make them do what I thought they should do. I am amazed at my own audacity as I tried to control God and my children. The presumption of thinking that I knew better than anyone else, including God. Now I am less judgmental and pray less out of fear. I mostly listen.

Some days my prayer is one of gratitude. The law of attraction is that we get more of what we focus on. When I focus on all the good things in my life and feel the gratitude of that, I get more of these good things.

On occasion I have felt so good that momentarily I thought, "I feel so good today that I do not need to pray or meditate." My prayer on that day should be, "Thank you, God, that I am already feeling You today."

On those days when I am in a negative state of mind, and do not feel good (or God) I tell myself, "I choose to step back into the light of God and feel His divine presence now." He had not moved. I had moved. He has not abandoned me. I have allowed something to block the Light.

Sometimes I sit quietly and focus on my breathing. Occasionally music will help me arrive at the quiet place I am seeking. If I only have a minute or two, I just use that short time to feel the sacred quiet, and then I am off to my day. When I have more time and I have a problem or question, I ask the question and then put it aside and just listen without expectation of an immediate answer. Sometimes the answer is immediate, and sometimes it comes later in an unexpected way.

I often use journaling to gain understanding of myself. I can be clueless and begin to journal, and the answers and understandings will end up on paper. Journaling to gain self-understanding is different than journaling to keep a record of the events of your life. Journaling to gain self-awareness is about writing your feelings, both positive and negative. It is about recording your insights. It is about recording your dreams which can help you understand the workings of your sub-conscious mind. It is about asking questions and getting answers. You can write your question and then sit quietly and wait for an answer. Trust what comes to you.

Another way to get answers is to write your question with your dominant hand (right for most of us) and then switch your pen to the other hand and just start writing. This accesses your subconscious mind. You will be amazed at what you will write.

If I have a wandering mind and an abundance of busy thoughts spoiling my hoped-for quiet as I am meditating, I forgive myself and ask the thoughts to just pass through. For me, every meditation is different, and I strive to accept what *is*, and just allow.

When I pray for myself and others, I no longer try to manipulate others or the situation. I once had a close friend who was having problems in her marriage. There were children involved, and my heart went out to all of them. My prayers in times past would have probably been to ask God to bless them not to get a divorce. I would have also interjected my judgements of the situation based solely on what I heard from my friend. I would have instructed God how to solve the problem. I have a different understanding now. My prayer now is one of sending love, understanding, and comfort. I ask that whatever serves their highest good will transpire. Then I just sit and ask if there is anything else I should ask for them. If something else does come to mind, I ask for that.

Sometimes I am not sure what to pray. I simply ask what I should pray. Whatever comes to mind, that is what I pray. The answers are always given. Ask and learn to listen. Often someone who is sick, injured, or going through a hard time will ask me to pray for them. I *always* ask them, "What exactly do you want me to ask God for?" Whatever they say they want is exactly what I ask in my prayer. Sometimes I am surprised at what they want. Some will say they want to be healed completely. Others will say they just do not want to die at this time or want to be able to deal with the disease. I totally honor what the person wants. I believe God does too.

Throughout Christian scripture the three words *ask, believe,* and *receive* are repeated in that order over and over, leading one to believe that what we ask for, and believe we will receive, we *will* receive. I believe that we always get what we ask for, although much of what we ask for is done unconsciously. We are often unaware of what we are *asking for* on the unconscious level. Have you ever heard a parent say to a misbehaving child, "You are asking for it!" What the parent means is that the child is asking for some type of punishment. The child is not saying "Give me a spanking!" but he is *unaware* that his behavior is *asking* for punishment. So we could say that the child is *unconsciously* asking for something unpleasant. We are all this way. If we receive something we think we really do not want, look a little deeper and find the unconscious thing we asked for and received.

Staying Connected

In my backyard is a pear tree. Mowing with a small tractor one day, I got too close and broke a limb. It was not completely broken, and I wondered if the limb would die. This was several years ago, and the limb is still green and healthy and produces just as many good pears as the other limbs on this tree. Because the limb is still connected enough to get nutrients from its source, the tree, it still lives and is just as productive as ever. We are like the limb of the pear tree. As long as we stay connected to our Source, we are still spiritually healthy and productive.

I have another tree in my front yard which also suffered a broken limb. This limb however, was totally broken away from its source. I was amazed at how quickly all signs of life left the once beautiful branch. So it is with us. As long as we *stay connected* to our Source, we live and thrive because we continue to get life-giving nutrients. Prayer and meditation are two ways to keep us connected to *our* Source.

Trust

One of the most important things we can learn and teach our children is trust. When we are born into this world we are open and naturally trusting. We lose this innate trust as we experience life. We are taught by well-meaning adults not to trust. "Do not talk to strangers. Do not trust anyone you do not know. Do as you are told." Without realizing it, our teachers, religious leaders, and parents taught us to close down our innate ability to trust *ourselves*.

Trust is reliance upon the Divine, and the divine is in us. I believe that is what it means in Psalms 118:8, "It is better to trust in the Lord than to put confidence in man." Proverbs 3:5-6 also reads, "Trust in the Lord with all thine heart: and lean not unto thine own understanding. In all thy ways acknowledge Him, and He shall direct thy paths." What a gift to know the truth of all things. You have it in you to know what to do about your life, not just some things, but *all* things. And guess what? So do children. Just imagine how that could free you from worry when you guide and teach your child how to go within to know all things. Imagine the peace and confidence your children will have. Think of all the sexual abuse that could be deterred by a child being able to feel inside themselves that *something is not right here*. The implications are endless. **Trusting the divine within is the most empowering teaching we can give to our children.** It is the most empowering thing we can learn in our own lives.

Some time ago in teaching a Life Skills class (see section on Skills for Life) in my community, I was teaching this principle. There were the usual questions and comments and resistance to this new idea that we can trust the divine in ourselves and others. A woman raised her hand to tell the following story:

"In 1977, I was just out of college and took a flight to a distant city to interview for a job. I was prepared with plenty of money in traveler's checks. When I approached the rental car company, I discovered that they would not take my traveler's checks. The rental car could only be secured with a credit card, and I did not have one. The man behind me, seeing my distress, offered his credit card. I gratefully accepted. I drove the three hours to my job interview, completed the interview, and then drove back to the car rental company and paid my debt using my traveler's checks. I never realized until now what a gift this stranger had given me. He trusted me. I knew I would not take advantage of his trust in me. I am still amazed at his kindness."

We can only speculate what the man was thinking or why he chose to trust enough to risk letting a stranger use his credit card. I do know that the divine in him could know that this woman would not misuse his credit card and that she would repay her debt. I know that the divine in her could trust him and that she could know that it was safe for her to trust the divine in this stranger. It is also evident that this display of trust in the divine between total strangers brought out the very best in them both. It brought out the divine.

If you find yourself in a similar situation as this man, should you let a stranger use your credit card? Only if you go inside yourself and hear, *"Yes."* You can know what to do in every situation. The divine can also warn not to do so if that is needed.

When my children were young, my sons were involved in sports. At the end of the season, the team and their families were given a skating party. My sons who played on the team were eight and ten at the time. My husband and I decided to make a quick trip to the nearby mall leaving these two boys, along with their six-year-old brother and twelve-year-old sister, there in the safety of this private party. A little voice inside said, "You might want to stay here." At this time in my life, I was not sure if it was the voice of the Divine or the voice of my fear. I convinced myself that I was being overprotective, and we left. When we arrived at the mall, we were paged. Samuel had broken his leg and was at the hospital. If I had stayed at the skating rink, would Samuel still have broken his leg? Probably. Would Samuel (and Mom) have felt a lot better if Mom and Dad had been there? Yes. The divine was telling me, but I confused it with my fear.

When we clear our fears, we can hear the divine in surprising ways. A few years ago, my oldest daughter and her husband and children were attending her husband's family reunion 2,000 miles away. They do this annually, and I am always glad for them to be able to go. But for some reason I was unusually uneasy about this particular trip. It is my usual practice to pray for them and their safety, but I was not feeling any peace in my prayers. I just could not shake the apprehension I was feeling. I was also having flashes of seeing my oldest granddaughter, Dallas, crying. This was disturbing, to say the least. The thought came into my mind to ask for a legion of angels to be on guard around Dallas. I asked them to protect Dallas and everyone at the reunion. Having done this, I was much more at peace. During the two weeks they were gone, I occasionally had a little fear creep in and would immediately see in my mind the legion of angels. There was no phone service where they were and I did not hear from them until they returned home.

When they returned I got a call from my daughter, and she was telling me all about the trip. After listening to how much fun they had, I asked her if Dallas was okay. She hesitated and then said, "As a matter of fact, she almost drowned." She went on to say that only the adults were to go white-water rafting, but since her husband's brother is a skilled river guide, they decided to let the kids go rafting as well. The water was swift, and the raft dumped some of the kids out. Dallas had on a life preserver and is a good swimmer, but the water kept pulling her under. Her dad and uncles frantically tried to reach her. Miraculously they were able to pull her to safety. For days after, Dallas would cry when the incident was mentioned. I am grateful that this time I did not mistake the divine in me for fear. I recognized the divine promptings and was guided with exactly what to do.

A few weeks ago I traveled out of town to visit a friend. The plan was to get up early on Sunday morning and drive the five-hour trip home. We awoke to an unexpected snow on the ground that morning, and there was more snow predicted midday on the roads I was to travel. Some roads were already closed. Had I used my logical mind, I would have stayed with my friend another day or two until the roads cleared, but my inner guidance said to wait until late morning and then leave. My logical mind and my inner guidance argued slightly, but I left at 10:30 a.m. The predicted snow never came, and the temperature warmed enough to melt all the snow between my friend's home and mine. Hardly anyone was on the road because of the predicted midday snow.

I trusted my inner guidance, and the roads could not have been more safe.

Reclaim your power to receive constant personal guidance directly from the Divine. Teach and allow your child to trust the Divine that is within them. We are all more powerful than we realize.

Exercises
For Creating New Parenting Patterns

1. Develop a regular prayer or meditation routine that works for you.

2. Have a quiet time for the whole family once a day, even if it is only a few minutes.

3. Notice and journal times when you feel connected to God (Universe, Light, Nature, etc.).

4. Have a conversation with your child about TRUST as you understand it now.

5. List ways you can begin to teach your child about trust.

Section II

HELPING YOUR CHILD

I can be of no real help to another unless I see that the two of us are in this together. (Hugh Prather)

CHAPTER 4
All Are Equal

D o you remember when you were a child? How did you feel and think? Who was that person? How about when you were a teen? How about now? How about when you become eighty? Older people sometimes say they feel like the same person they were as a child or young person. They *are* the same person, the same spirit. The body changes. New experiences are added. But we are the same person. When you speak to a child, remember that he is the same person that in a few short years will be in a body that is the age that you are now. When you speak to an elderly person, they are the same person whose body, a few short years ago, was the age of yours. When we let ourselves be really conscious of this fact, we will have more respect for people of all ages. The three year old, the teen, the adult, the elderly; we are all equal.

"I can be of no real help to another unless I see that the two of us are in this together . . ." (Hugh Prather, from the forward of Gerald Jampolsky's book *Love is Letting Go of Fear)* This expresses a new paradigm which is one of personal responsibility and equality. We *are* in this together. The old paradigm of how to help someone is based on inequality. I may see myself as *inferior* because I have a problem such as drug addiction, a failing marriage, or an illness. I then look to someone else, who I see as *superior* and knowing more or as having skills that I lack, to fix my problem. The person I look to sees himself as being superior to me. By focusing his skills on my problem and removing it, it is no longer my problem. I gave the responsibility for it over to him, and he then tells me what to think and what to do.

Does the medical doctor warrant more respect than the grade school teacher, the Wal-Mart stock boy, the garbage man, or a child? Miss getting your garbage to the curb even once, and you will quickly realize the contribution of the garbage man. I like having my garbage hauled away every week. If my garbage did not get picked up for a month, I would *really* be aware of the important contribution of the people who perform this under-appreciated service.

Sadly, it seems to be the disposition of many who are in a position of authority to exercise deplorable behavior towards those over whom they are given jurisdiction. It is misunderstood and misused power.

I worked with an eight-year-old boy who was out of control. He would get upset at school and run out of the classroom or out of the school building. He was out of control at home as well. He was interviewed by a probation officer with the county juvenile court system. She showed him no respect at all as she attempted to "scare him" into appropriate behavior. She spoke loudly using profanity as she threatened him with incarceration. She showed no respect for this little boy who was troubled and hurting. He responded in like manner by yelling profanities back at the probation officer. This of course did not help matters. He was so upset when he was brought to me that he crawled under my desk and would not come out. He finally allowed me to crawl under the desk with him, and we did the session under the desk. He finally came out after we worked on this traumatic event.

Perhaps this probation officer was well meaning. Perhaps her methods succeed with some children by scaring them into behaving appropriately, but it shows no respect, no equality. Is the adult in a position of power to be respected more than a small troubled boy? Was there not a better way to help this child?

I make it a point to have the children I work with call me by my first name. I was taught as a child to call adults mister or misses to show respect. It was considered disrespectful to call an adult by their first name. If we view the child as an equal and have mutual respect for them, should we not either both be on a first-name basis or both call each other mister or miss? I have always felt respected by any child who has called me by my first name.

In Dr. Suess' book *Horton Hears a Who*, Horton says, "A person's a person no matter how small." This is a profound statement. When a parent, teacher, or other adult views a child as equal and a meaningful contributor in the relationship, it changes us, and it changes the child. Think of a time when a child in your life said or did something profound. "Out of the mouth of babes" is often said when wise words come from the mouth of a child, but it is usually treated as if it is a one-time thing and out of the ordinary. We react as if it is a rarity, and we do not expect any other profoundness to come from such a little person.

What can a small baby contribute? Nothing brings a smile to the face of an adult more than when they see a baby. I have watched a sleeping baby in a mall. It is rare for anyone to walk by without looking at the baby and smiling. That is one contribution babies make . . . bringing a moment of joy to us as we pass by.

Think of a time when you felt that you were not a meaningful contributor or had nothing important to give. This can cause feelings of "I'm not good enough," "I'm not important," "I don't matter," "I can't do anything." It can cause discouragement and even despair. Now think of a time when your contribution, even a kind word or a smile, was appreciated and made a difference to someone. This can cause a sense of self-confidence, happiness, joy, and a feeling of "I matter," and "I have purpose." You will then most likely feel inspired to look for ways to continue to be a contributor.

When I was a young mother years ago, I was not only overwhelmed with the endless duties of caring for my children, but for some reason at that time in my life I was bombarded with thoughts of the inhumanity of mankind. I remember asking myself one morning, "Are there any decent people in the world? Can I trust anyone?" As I got out of my car at a department store with a baby in my arms, a two year old holding on to my leg with an untied shoe, and a four year old by the hand, I needed to tie the shoe of my two year old. I thought, "I just can't do this." A man in his sixties was walking past. He hesitated, then asked if he could help. He tied my child's shoe, I thanked him, and he was on his way. He will never know how he not only gave me a hand with tying my toddler's shoe, but he was the answer to my troubling question earlier in the day. It was such a small thing he did that day, but it was a huge contribution to my world.

Look at everyone you meet as if they have something wonderful to contribute, because they do: the co-worker, the grumpy lady checking you out at the grocery store, the teenager with the blue spiked hair, the person who comes from a far away place. Look at yourself, the self no one really knows. We are all the same. See the glorious reflection of divinity in every person in your life, every person who crosses your path. We are all in this together. If there is hope for this world, it is in seeing everyone as no better than or no less than anyone else.

If you have a hard time seeing a child as equal to you, take some time to get down on their level. Look them in the eye. Ask questions. LISTEN to the answers. Think deeply about the answers they give. Remember when you were a child. Remember how you felt, how you wanted to be regarded. Remember what you knew that no one realized, and what you wanted someone to acknowledge in you. Look beyond the inexperienced childishness, and look deeply and see the child-like wisdom, the unconditional love, the joy, and the profound contribution of this human being. I recently went to the movies with my grandchildren. The best part of the movie was hearing my granddaughter laugh from the very core of her being. I would have been content with not watching the movie at all but to just feel the joy of a child's laughter. Everyone contributes. Everyone. Just look. You will see it.

Everything Is Okay

I few years ago, I was in my car headed to a discount wallpaper store. With me was my then three-year-old granddaughter. It was great fun for her to be going out with Meemee, and I must admit, it was great fun for me as well. For her it was my mostly undivided attention and an afternoon of being away from home doing big-girl stuff like shopping and going out to eat. For me it was one-on-one time with one of the most precious little beings I have ever had the privilege of knowing.

I had heard that being a grandparent was much more fun than being a parent. And here I was, having a blast with a three year old. I hung on every word that came from her young but wise mouth. Funny how I listened more to her than I did to my own children when they were small. I was so busy trying to be the perfect parent, teaching them everything I thought they needed to know, that I missed a great lesson. These little beings are here not only for me to protect and care for and teach, but to teach me as well.

As we drove along looking for the wallpaper store, I knew I was close, but I took a wrong turn.

"I took a wrong turn, Dallas. I know we're close. I'll turn this way this time."

"That's okay, Meemee. It's okay, right, Meemee? It's okay if you take a wrong turn. You'll find the right turn, right, Meemee?"

"Yeah, we'll just keep looking, keep turning. We'll find it. No big deal."

As I listened to her telling me over and over that *it's okay*, I recalled all the times I had said that to her. When she was learning to walk and would fall down, "It's okay. Just try it again." When she would spill her drink, "It's okay. Let's just clean it up." When she would cry because she was sad, "It's okay. Just cry it all out and then go play and be happy again." We were teaching each other. We were empowering ourselves with the belief that everything is okay because everything really is okay.

Treating your own mistakes and those of your child as something different than okay brings feelings of guilt, shame, regret, blame, and sadness. Another word that is used in our culture is SIN. For many, the word sin brings up feelings of guilt and shame. However, the word sin in the Greek language means *to miss the mark*. That is exactly what sin or a mistake is. It is just something that did not work. We missed the mark. "There are no mistakes or failures, only lessons." (Denis Waitley) Everything is just an experience from which to learn and grow and to reevaluate and consider how to change it or do it differently so that it works better, so that it brings happiness into our lives instead of unhappiness and dysfunction.

Remember seeing a child take his first steps learning to walk. At first he falls down more than he walks. Every time he falls down, he gets back up. I have never heard a parent scold a child for falling down as he is learning to walk. What I have seen many times is family gathered around cheering the child on with words of encouragement. Criticism would be ridiculous. It would take the joy out of the experience for the child as well as the parent. It would hinder the process of learning to walk and be self-sufficient. It would also start a pattern of "I can never do anything right" or "when I try I get criticized."

No matter what age your child is, look at everything he or she does as if they were learning to walk. Cheer them on with words of encouragement. Potty training, school work, making a bed, everything. And give yourself words of encouragement when you miss the mark. You are learning, too.

All Experience Is for Our Learning

Imagine every experience being treated the same as learning to walk. Here is a story of one mother who learned how to do that.

It was almost 11 p.m. I had been asleep for an hour or so. My nineteen-year-old son lightly knocked on the bedroom door. "Mom?"

He was in college and still living at home. He had been out with his girlfriend and just gotten home. He was a good kid. He came and went as he pleased and never stayed out very late. "Mom . . ." I was a little disoriented being awakened at this hour, and I couldn't tell what he was saying.

"Open the door and come on in so I can hear you," I said as I tried to wake myself up. The door opened.

"Come on over," I said. He kneeled by the edge of the bed as I sat up and became more awake. "What's wrong?"

"Mom, I took some natural diet pills. I don't know what's happening. I'm afraid to go to sleep. I'm afraid if I do . . . I won't wake up."

Earlier in my life I would probably have immediately started to judge and criticize. I used to think it was my job as a responsible mother to point out to him that he had done something very stupid. But I had learned to look at things differently, and tonight I was able to be helpful instead of harmful.

We walked downstairs. He told me the whole story. He had been overweight most of his childhood and had lost a significant amount of weight from about age thirteen to sixteen. But he had issues with the weight, and even though he was slim and handsome, he still looked at himself as fat.

He and his girlfriend had argued about going to the health food store. She knew he did not need the diet aid. The clerk had taken one look at him, and she too told him he did not need them. But he took them anyway.

He had taken the recommended dose. When he did not feel any different, he took more. That had been several hours ago, and his heart was still beating fast. He felt exhausted but was afraid to sleep. And he felt far away.

"I know it was a stupid thing to do, but will you stay with me for a while?" He was really scared, and my heart went out to him. We went into the living room.

"You lay here on the couch. I won't leave. I'll stay with you all night if you need me to." He lay on the couch, and I put my hands on his back near the bottom of his spine. It was icy cold. I felt my own fear surface and then leave. I sat with my hands on him for a while. Warmth returned, and

he went peacefully to sleep. I lay down on the other couch staying awake for a while longer. He woke up momentarily and told me he was okay and that I could go back to bed.

The next morning I took the opportunity to tell him I was glad he woke me up and that I was glad he was okay and not to beat himself up about what he had done, that it is just an experience from which to learn. He thanked me again and gave everyone in the family a hug and told us he loved us. He was glad to be alive.

This story is a great example of how a parent can respond when a child misses the mark. This young man did not need to be told he had done something foolish. He already knew that and acknowledged it. He needed love and support. He needed just exactly what his mother gave him.

Exercises
For Creating New Parenting Patterns

1. Speak to someone new today as you look at them as your equal. Journal your feelings about it.

2. List ways that your child contributes.

3. List new ways you can encourage your child to contribute. [not a list of chores:)]

4. Have a conversation with your child. Ask questions and LISTEN to them as though they were a very wise soul. What profound thing did they say?

Honor your child's feelings and teach them to
express their emotions in appropriate ways.

CHAPTER 5
Stress in Children

Emotions

We all experience a wide range of emotions. It is part of being human. We are emotional beings. The following list of emotions are from Ester and Jerry Hicks' book *Ask and It Is Given*. The higher on the scale the emotion is, the higher the vibration, resulting in physical and emotional health and happiness. The lower on the scale, the lower the vibration resulting in dis-ease and unhappiness.

1. Joy / Knowledge / Empowerment / Freedom /Love / Appreciation
2. Passion
3. Enthusiasm / Eagerness / Happiness
4. Positive Expectation / Belief
5. Optimism
6. Hopefulness
7. Contentment
8. Boredom
9. Pessimism
10. Frustration / Irritation / Impatience
11. "Overwhelment"
12. Disappointment
13. Doubt
14. Worry
15. Blame
16. Discouragement
17. Anger
18. Revenge
19. Hatred / Rage
20. Jealousy
21. Insecurity / Guilt / Unworthiness
22. Fear / Grief / Depression / Despair / Powerlessness

To see how your emotions affect how you feel, do the following: start at the bottom of the scale and think of a time when you felt that emotion. Then move up to the next one and remember a time when you felt that way. Continue until you move all the way up to the top one. This is a quick way to experience how our emotions affect us.

Stuffed Emotions

There are two books I use constantly whose authors have done extensive work on how our emotions affect us. Both books have a comprehensive list of illnesses and dis-eases in the body and the probable emotion that can cause them. Louise Hay's *You Can Heal Your Life and Heal Your Body* and Karol K. Truman's *Feelings Buried Alive Never Die* are an excellent place to start for an understanding of how emotions affect us. The Rapid Eye Institute also has a body chart showing where negative emotions are stored in the body. You can download it free by going to www.rapideyetechnology.com.

Negative emotions should be felt, acknowledged, and let go. Children come into the world knowing how to do this. But soon after they arrive, they are taught:

- Don't cry.
- Big boys/girls don't cry.
- Dry up those tears.
- It's not nice to be angry.
- You shouldn't feel that way.
- There is nothing to be afraid of.
- Here. Have some ice cream. It will make you feel better.

Suppressed emotions stay in the body. They cause illness, discomfort, unhappiness, and negative patterns of behavior. Honor your child's feelings. Allow them to feel their emotions and let them know it is okay to feel whatever they feel.

Peace

I have a chart of negative and positive emotions with appropriate faces that I use in my RET practice with children. Some of the negative emotions are angry, sad, hurt, jealous, shy, hate, and worry. Positive emotions are happy, joyful, loved, peace, and confident. I sometimes ask them to pick the feeling they have been experiencing a lot lately and then pick what they would like to trade it in for. The majority of the time, kids of all ages, regardless of the negative emotion they have been experiencing, will choose *peace* as the feeling they would like to feel. This really surprised me. At first I was not sure if they knew what peace really meant. Well, they do, and it is what they want. Jesus is quoted to have said, *"Peace* I leave with you, peace I give unto you . . . Let not your heart be *troubled,* neither let it be *afraid."* (John 14:27) It seems that Jesus was telling us that we could trade in our trouble and fear for peace.

Fear, anger, sadness, hurt, or any other negative emotion will block our feelings of peace. Any time we are out of alignment with who we really are—which is whole and perfect and unconditional love—we will experience an unsettled, disharmonious feeling. For me it feels like my insides are trembling or like I am off center. When I feel peace, I feel centered, connected to God and to the earth and its inhabitants, in harmony with myself, and still.

Tools to Release Stress and Negative Emotions

1. Expressing

One of the best ways to help our children release negative feelings is to provide them with an environment to freely express what they are feeling without judgement or punishment. Learning to listen is a skill well worth the effort.

Sometimes the child needs a little coaching to "get it all out." The story goes that a young girl was playing with neighborhood children, and a vicious dog bit one of the children. This was very traumatic for the girl to witness. The girl ran home to the mother crying and could hardly talk. The mother asked questions to get the girl to tell about it. "What happened? Who was there? What did the dog look like? How big was the dog? How did you feel? What did you do? What did the other kids do?" After the girl told every detail, the mother had her tell it all over again. After about the third time, the emotion of the event was gone, and it was now just a story. The girl's response to telling it again was now "Can I go play now?" At this point it is best for the parent not to bring it up again unless the child brings it up. The initial expressing releases the emotion of the event. Any continued rehashing of the event can cause the child to get stuck in the reliving of the old trauma.

2. Holding a Space

In working with clients in my Rapid Eye practice, I meet many wonderful people with an assortment of emotional issues that have caused varying degrees of unhappiness or dysfunction in their lives. Some have experienced horrendous abuse, others have lived in dysfunctional families, and still others do not know why their lives are not working for them. What I have experienced is that what *everyone* needs is to be listened to with compassion and without judgement. I call it *holding a space.* I feel it is my number one job with my clients. They cannot feel free enough to look at and let go of their deep—seeded negative emotions without first being heard. Many of them have never been honored in this way. Some have never uttered out loud their traumatic experience. Others have spoken but have not been truly listened to without judgement. One woman I worked with came to tears and said, "No one ever just listened to me before. No one ever listened or responded with love." She was able for the first time to speak and be heard and release the buried negative emotions she had carried since childhood.

Yvonne and Rich St. John-Dutra have a wonderful program for high school students called Challenge Day that has been very successful for teens. One of the techniques they use is explained in their book, *Be the Hero You've Been Waiting For.* They have the teen say, "I'm angry that . . . ," and every time they express something they are angry about, the *coach* says, "What else?" The key here is to just listen without judgement, without getting upset, without giving advice, to just let them express. You can find out more about their program or order their book at www. challengeday.org.

Each of us, young and old, want to be heard. Start listening to your children. Hold a space for them. Let them express. Allow it to be okay to let the words of anger, hurt, sadness, hate, and frustration be spoken. In speaking them, the negative emotions can be released. If left unexpressed those emotions become stuffed down inside to cause problems later. Resist the urge to preach or sermonize. Resist the urge to be defensive or take it personal.

Resist the urge to think you can tell them how to solve their problem. Just listen . . . with love. Be present and hold the space for them to feel safe enough to express in your presence and let them feel your unconditional love.

3. Crying

If a child is hurt or upset, let them cry. Crying is a great way to release physical or emotional pain. Acknowledging their hurt and allowing them to express it through tears is very healthy. You can often help the most by saying nothing. Hold them or put your arms around them if they want you to and just let them cry. Never tell them they *should not* feel that way. The fact is, they hurt, either physically or emotionally. Honor their feelings and let them express it. If you feel your child is just being a "baby" and trying to get attention, do some soul searching (probably at a time other than during this event) and ask yourself, "What is going on with the child?" Suppressing tears suppresses negative emotions that will not go away. It will cause problems later.

There are some children who tend to get stuck in their crying and negativity. A good way to handle this, after you have honored what they feel and allowed them to express through talking and crying, is the following. Tell them they need to cry more and louder to get it all out. Tell them to cry as loud as they can. Then tell them you are going to count to ten, and it will all be gone. As you count, if they want to stop or are not crying loudly, encourage them to keep it up until you get to ten. Then tell them, "Great job! Now it's all gone!" They will probably be all cried out and feeling good again.

Another thing that works well with children is to direct the pain to go somewhere else. An example is a child who has fallen down and skinned her knee. Crying and maybe a band-aide may work fine, but if it does not, do the following. Ask them if they want to send the pain somewhere. Occasionally they want to hold on to the pain, but if they say yes, put one hand on the knee (or near the knee if touching it hurts) and tell the child, "The pain is going to go in my hand, up my arm, across my chest, down my other arm and out my hand. Where do you want to send the pain?" It could be sent to a tree or the ground or anywhere the child chooses. Then direct slowly with your finger the pain energy going in one hand and out the other. One time I did this with my grandchild, and we sent it to Grandpa. Grandpa gladly accepted it and danced with it, and everyone including the child had a good laugh. Energy follows thought, and we have the power to re-direct the pain energy wherever we choose. This little exercise also teaches the child that they have power to control and direct their own life.

However, often the continued crying can be because of other previous events similar to the current one, and a pattern can be created. Ask them, "Do you remember a time when you felt this way before?" or "What else are you crying about?" I believe they always know the answer to this, and asking these questions can help them express previous hurts. If they say they do not know, ask them to guess. Let them know it does not matter if they get it right or wrong, that it is just a guess. It has been my experience with children and adults that the answer they "guess" is usually exactly right.

4. Physical activity

It is a well-known fact, that exercise is a stress reliever and also helps with depression. I often tell the children I work with that one way they can release anger and other negative feelings is to punch their pillow and scream. Going outside and stomping their feet or running around the house a couple of times is another way to physically get it out of the body. This is especially good for children who are aggressive and experience a lot of anger and act out in a physical way. This teaches them positive ways to be physical. Children who exhibit anger usually have deep sadness under that anger that needs to be addressed.

5. Drawing Pictures

I use drawing in my practice with children a lot. Many times the child can express what he is feeling by drawing easier than by talking. Sometimes children do not have the vocabulary to express what they are feeling. Sometimes they are not ready to acknowledge what happened, or they do not know how they feel about it. Usually the story in the picture is the child's story.

One little girl came to me because her mother was concerned about a sudden dislike for school. She did not want to talk about it. At the beginning of the session, I asked her to make up a story about Eli (a puppet I use in my practice) who did not want to go to school anymore. She told her own story beautifully by making the story about Eli. It makes it less threatening when the story is about someone else. When she finished drawing, I had her tell me about the picture. It was one of Eli feeling sad and embarrassed because the teacher had gotten on to him. The teacher had spoken harshly to Eli. At the end of the session, I had her take the same picture and add or change anything in the picture to show how school will be for Eli now that the story has been expressed and the negative emotion released. She added lots of yellow marks and then other bright-colored marks on the paper that she said represented light and happy feelings around Eli and the teacher. I suggested she draw pink light to represent love, swirling all around the school room, Eli, the teacher and all the kids, and even in the hall-ways and going in and out of the windows. It was a beautiful picture. She was delighted with it. She took the picture home to show her parents, which was a great way to express herself to her parents about the situation. She even took it to school, and when the teacher asked her about it, she explained all about Eli's experience. According to her mother, her enjoyment of school returned immediately and has not changed to this day.

6. Stuffed Animals and Puppets

I use puppets a lot in my practice to communicate with children. Scruffy Dog is another lovable puppet the children enjoy. I will ask questions to Scruffy Dog, and then I tell the child to listen to the puppet whisper the answer to them. If I know the child is experiencing anger, I will say, "Scruffy is really mad today, but he doesn't want to tell me about it. Maybe he will tell you about it." The child may pick up the puppet and say, "What's wrong Scruffy? Why are you mad?" Then they will put the puppet to his ear and listen intently. At this point, whatever the child says is the child's story and what the child is feeling. This is a way to let them express themselves when they are not ready to come right out with it. I once had a boy who was very shy who responded very well to the puppets. One week to my surprise he proudly brought with him his own stuffed animal, a very large gorilla. The gorilla wanted a session! With your own children, a favorite doll or teddy bear could be used this way. My granddaughter told us an elaborate story of her extended family, using about a dozen or so dolls and stuffed animals. We all had great fun with it and learned a lot about her perspective of our family.

7. Deep Breathing

Have you ever noticed that when you are scared, mad, or nervous you hold your breath? When you catch yourself doing this, you can help yourself feel better by taking a few deep breaths. Also if you are tired and your energy seems to have left you, try taking a few really deep breaths. You will feel more energized. Dozing off at a boring meeting? A deep breath will not make the meeting any better, but it will keep you awake.

Remind your children to breathe deeply if you see them holding their breath. With a small child, have them blow something, like leaves, feathers, or bubbles. It is fun for them, and they will feel better instantly. You can tell them to blow their anger into the bubbles and then watch as the bubbles burst and let the anger go. Make it fun.

8. Eye Movement

One of the many eye movements used in the Rapid Eye Technology model is moving the eyes laterally. You can have your child do this while they tell you what they are feeling. Just have them move their eyes as far as they can to one side and then as far as they can to the other side, back and forth in a zig zag as you have them say "I release the anger (sadness, fear, or whatever they feel)." You can say the words along with them if they want you to. Go to www.rapideyetechnology.com/selfcare.htm to see a demonstration of how to do this.

9. Emotional Freedom Technique (EFT) or Tapping

I teach everyone I work with how to do a technique called tapping. It is one of the best emotional release techniques available. It is easy to learn and a quick way to feel better instantly. It is based on the work of Gary Craig. The Rapid Eye Institute has incorporated this wonderful tool into the RET model because of the effectiveness of it. The EFT web site is www.emofree. com. You can download a free copy of their manual. *Good Bye Ouchies and Grouchies, Hello Happy Feelings: EFT for Kids of All Ages* by Lynne Namka is another great resource for teaching this technique to kids. This book is also a great aid in teaching kids about their feelings.

Tapping is very simple. It will even stop a panic attack. If you are upset with your child and want to release the anger so you can calmly address the situation, you can take a moment to do this technique, and then you can deal calmly with your child. This is the very best technique you can use on yourself to release negative emotions. See Appendage C at the back of this book for an explanation of how to do this technique. If you have trouble learning to use it, any RET technician or EFT technician can easily teach it to you.

I worked with a six-year-old boy who had some anger and sadness about his father's abandonment of the family. He was having chest pains, and the doctors could not find anything physically wrong with him. He also was afraid to leave his mother to go to school. He did well in school and liked school, but he would panic and cry when it came time to leave for school. In his RET session we addressed the issues about his father leaving. When it was time to go to school, the anxiety was better but still a problem. I taught him and his mother the tapping, and they did it in the morning before school on whatever he was feeling. He was then able to go to school without fear and anxiety.

10. Visualizations

"Imagination is everything. It is the preview of life's coming attractions." (Albert Einstein) It is well documented that athletes who visualize themselves hitting a home run, ringing a basket, or jumping hurdles have more success than those who do not. The brain fires up the exact same way whether the event is real or imagined. You are just as scared when you *think* the movement in the woods is a bear as you would be if it *really was* a bear. Physiologically, you react the same way: heart racing, shallow breathing, sweaty hands.

A story that demonstrates the profound benefit of visualization is from Josh Waitzkin, eight-time national chess champion and martial arts champion, holding numerous national and world championship titles. In his book *The Art of Learning*, he tells of preparing for a national competition. He broke his right hand six weeks before the competition. The hand was in a cast up to his elbow, and the doctor said there was no way he could compete. The cast would come off just a few days before competition. The bone could heal in six weeks, but the muscles would atrophy. It would be absurd to consider taking tournament-level impact under those conditions. But he was resolved to compete. He continued to practice developing the use of his left hand to an advantage. After every exercise set with the left hand, he visualized the workout passing to the muscles on the right, which was in the cast. He could feel the energy flowing into the unused muscles. When the cast was removed four days before the competition, the doctor was stunned. There was hardly any atrophy of the muscles in the right hand and arm. He was cleared to compete and won the national competition.

Visualization works well with kids. Have them *imagine* a new or better way to do something. If they are nervous about the first day of school, you could have them close their eyes and imagine walking confidently into the school and seeing their friends and teacher smile. Have them imagine everything going well. If there is something of which they are especially fearful, have them visualize it in a way that feels right to them.

You can use visualization after something unpleasant has happened. Perhaps your child had an unpleasant situation with a friend. After hearing the story, and using any other tools needed to release the negative emotion of the event (tapping, expressing, or one of the other techniques explained in this chapter), have them close their eyes and imagine the story happening another way with a different outcome. You will be surprised at how this will positively affect all concerned.

Another way to use visualization is after the child is asleep and in REM (rapid eye movement) sleep. They will go into REM about an hour after they go to sleep. You will notice their eyes flutter under their eyelids.

Six-year-old Dylan was extremely upset about his dog, Pinch, getting hit by a car and dying. His mother could not get him to talk about it, so I suggested that she talk to him in his sleep. I wrote a visualization which she used as a guideline, changing or adding anything directed by her own personal guidance. To give you an example of what can be done, I have included that visualization here.

Visualization for Dylan and Pinch

"Dylan"

Tell him the following in your own words:

- *How much you love him*
- *How special he is*
- *That he is safe*
- *That it is okay to feel whatever he feels*

Then:

"I know how much you loved Pinch. Pinch loved you too. It's okay to be sad that Pinch died. It's okay to feel whatever you feel. How do you feel about Pinch dying?" (Pause)

"Just gather up all those sad or mad feelings you have about Pinch and see them." Use your own intuition here on what his feelings might be.

"Those feelings are kind of dark, smokey." Use words he will understand.

"Now just send those dark, heavy, or sad feelings to the light." (Pause)

"As they go into the light, watch them change into something white and sparkly." Use words he'll understand. (Pause)

"Now, watch them rain back down on you, making you feel all warm and good inside." (Pause)

"Dylan, Pinch is okay. He misses you. But he wants you to know that he is okay. Notice that he is in a bright, warm light. See Pinch. He is

running around and happy to see you. He is not hurt any more. He looks just the way he always did. His little body that was all hurt (whatever fits) is all good as new. Pinch is perfect. He misses you, but he is with the angels." Use words that fit your belief system. (Pause)

"Dylan, Pinch wants you to talk to him. Whatever you would like to say to Pinch, say that to him now." (Long pause)

"Dylan, Pinch has something to say to you. Even though Pinch couldn't talk before, he can tell you something now. Listen to Pinch." (Long pause)

"Dylan, are you ready to let Pinch go into the light with the angels? Good. Watch happy, playful (whatever fits) Pinch go off with the angels." (Pause)

"Sleep well, Dylan. When you wake up in the morning, you will be happy (add your own positive feelings) because you will remember all the good memories you have of Pinch and all the fun you had with him. Now you know that Pinch is okay."

Dylan's mother reported that after this he was much happier and would now speak of happy memories of Pinch.

11. Anchoring

Anchoring can be either negative or positive. An example of negative anchoring is hitting or spanking a child while telling them something negative, like "What you did was wrong" or "I hate you." An example of positive anchoring is when the child has done or said something good, like "Mom, thanks for helping me with my homework," and you give them a hug or touch them in a loving way. It is more than positive reinforcement. Anything that is said while touching the physical body in any way physically anchors the words and the feelings of the words into the body. Be very careful when consoling a grieving person. You do not want to anchor grief into their body. Consider expressing kind words and recalling happy memories and using touch to anchor that into the body by squeezing their hand or touching them in some appropriate way.

Exercises
For Creating New Parenting Patterns

1. List some of the negative things you were taught about emotions as a child that you have passed down to your child, such as big boys don't cry. Have a conversation with your child and explain that you would like for the two of you to work together to change this belief.

2. For the next eleven days, practice each of the eleven tools from this chapter. For example, on day one focus on and practice number one, expressing. On day two focus on and practice number two, holding a space.

Whatever we see in others is a mirror for us.

CHAPTER 6
Who is Teaching Whom?

Teacher and Student

Children teach us many things including how to be present and in the moment. If we remain open and notice, there is much more to learn from them. When I was raising my own children, I thought it was my job to teach, protect, correct, and mold them into responsible adults. I know I caused them a lot of pain. I constantly pointed out their imperfections so they could do better. I truly thought it was my job. What I have learned is that it is a two-way street. We teach each other. We help, love, and support each other. We are in this together. I believe there is something to learn from and teach to every person with whom we interact. We are both teacher and student. Children are no different. They both learn from us and teach us.

Mirrors

Whatever we see in others is a mirror for us. When I saw how my children could do better, I was really looking in the mirror and seeing how I needed to do better. When you see a fault in someone, just look for the mirror of that fault in you. It is always there. If you are irritated with something your spouse or anyone else does, ask yourself, "What is the mirror for me?" It is always there, and when we see it, we become more awake.

I became irritated with my husband because, as I told him, "You never take anything serious. Can't you just have a serious conversation with me? Do you always have to make a joke out of everything?" I really wanted to get the learning from this and to see the mirror. I did not get it at first. I *am* serious. *I* do not make a joke of everything. I have *lots* of serious conversations. Then it hit me. I am *too* serious. I need to lighten up! And when I did, a miracle happened. We began to have deeper, more serious conversations. When I *got it,* he no longer mirrored my behavior.

I hear lots of parents say, "Why are my kids always fighting and arguing?" I silently say, "How are you and your spouse getting along?" Do you see disrespectfulness in your child? Ask yourself, "How am I being disrespectful to my children or others?" As we see our reflection in our children (and others) one of two things will happen. Either they will give up the behavior because it will no longer be needed to teach us, or their behavior will no longer trigger a negative feeling in us. Learn the lessons. Your children are doing a great job teaching!

Mirroring is not just about negative behavior. Positive attributes are also mirrored. You cannot see in another what is not in you. There is an older man I have been acquainted with for many years. He is one of the most kind and loving people I know. When my daughter was in the "bratty teenager" stage (mirroring that for me I am sure) he did not seem to notice that behavior. He had unconditional love for everyone, even a rebellious teen. He always told me how wonderful she was. I thought he was blind at the time but appreciated his influence in her life. Now I realize they mirrored that for each other. He only had love, so that is what he saw in her. This magnified the love that was in her, that others missed.

Looking at everyone as a mirror for us, awakens us. It is not about blame or guilt or beating up on ourselves; it is about opening our eyes. It is about awakening. We can remain unconscious and live unskillfully and blindly, or we can wake up and live consciously and skillfully.

There is an interesting theory about birth order and the mirrors our children are for us. It goes like this:

- The first child mirrors the father's issues.
- The second child mirrors the mother's issues.
- The third child mirrors the parents' relationship.
- The fourth child mirrors the family relationships.
- If there are more than four children, it starts over. For example, the fifth child mirrors dad, sixth child mirrors mom, seventh mirrors parents' relationship, and the eighth mirrors family relationships.
- If there are five children, the fifth child mirrors father, mother, parents' relationship, and family relationships.
- If there is only one child, he takes on the job of mirroring all four issues (father's issues, mother's issues, parents' relationship, and family relationships).
- If there are two children, the first child mirrors father, second child mother, first child parents relationship, second child the family relationships.

It is very interesting to look at your children, yourself, and your siblings and see all the mirrors that are there for our learning.

I worked with a child in my Rapid Eye practice who was having problems at school and home. He was a very intelligent child, and he really came to understand himself and his behavior and made positive changes in his life. But there were some things he just would not change. At first I could not figure out why he was so resistant. He had made such amazing changes in other ways. Then I asked myself, "Who is he a mirror for?" He was the third child of four, which means he was the mirror for his parents' relationship. He was just doing his job of being a mirror! If both parents had been willing to work on their relationship, perhaps he could have completed his job of being their mirror.

Helping Children See Their Own Mirrors

When children get into disagreements or have a problem with another child, it is so easy for the parent or teacher to just gather the evidence, deliver the verdict, and solve the problem by siding with the child who is judged as right and punish the offender. Some parents approach these situations by just breaking up the fight and having everyone just go on with whatever they were doing before. No one learns anything with either of these approaches.

Ten-year-old John was sent out of the room for disrupting the class. The teacher asked me to talk with him. He was upset with another young man in his class named Jim and related to me what Jim had done. I first acknowledged John's feelings. He was upset, and we all have a right to feel whatever we feel. I then asked him to close his eyes and imagine what Jim was feeling and to guess why Jim had done what he had done. After a short time John's eyes popped open, and he looked like a light bulb had turned on in his head. He said, "Jim feels like no one likes him, and he doesn't think he has any friends. I have to go talk to him!" With that he bounded out the door and back to class. I never knew what was said between the two boys, but later that morning I saw them walking together like good friends. When a child looks at what the other child is feeling, they are really looking at a mirror of their own reflection. When this happens, they usually have real understanding and empathy and solve their own problems from this place instead of from a place of who is right and who is wrong.

When you live this principle of looking at the mirrors, a little coaching from time to time is all that is needed. Your child is on his way to becoming a conscious human being, dealing with his own challenges in a conscious way . . . all by himself.

Exercises
For Creating New Parenting Patterns

1. Think back over the last day or two. Remember a time when you were irritated at someone or when you found a fault in them. What is the mirror for you?

2. Think of the very best quality in your child. Now look at yourself. Find that quality in yourself.

3. What is your birth order in your family of origin? Whose issues do you mirror?

4. Notice a time when your child is in conflict and help him or her find the mirror for themselves by imagining what the other child is feeling.

Raising a child to know he is loved no matter what and that he is esteemed just because he exists is the essence of good self-esteem.

CHAPTER 7
Self-Esteem

Self-esteem is defined as *confidence in one's own worth*. There is much discussion on how to help a child get self-esteem. Many believe self-esteem and confidence are the results of a child *doing* something really well. We look at the good student, the captain of the football team, and the star ballerina as having good self-esteem. Perhaps they do. Many parents believe that their child must be successful in their endeavors such as school, sports, and dance to have good self-esteem. I believe that true self-esteem is the forerunner of successful endeavors, not the other way around. In the old paradigm, we are inferior to some and superior to others. In the new paradigm, we realize that true self-esteem comes from knowing that you are neither inferior nor superior to anyone.

Raising a child to know he is loved no matter what and that he is esteemed just because he exists is the essence of good self-esteem. "I love who you are, just the way you are. You don't have to BE anything other than who you are right now. You are loved and lovable." This is the message to give your child. If a child first knows he is loved and lovable, then he is free to discover his purpose in life and discover and express his talents in ways that create joy and abundance for himself and others.

Your Child is NOT Clay

Often parents try to mold a child into someone they perceive as important: athlete, scholar, or dancer. Children are encouraged to pursue certain careers: doctor, lawyer, teacher, or athlete. The parent is often well intentioned, wanting the child to be an important and happy person contributing in society. But you can no more mold a child into something he is not than you can change the color of his or her eyes.

Deepak Chopra, in *The Seven Spiritual Laws of Success,* says he told his children over and over again that there was a reason why they were here, and they had to find out what that reason was for themselves. He told them, "I never ever want you to worry about making a living. If you're unable to make a living when you grow up, I'll provide for you, so don't worry about that. I don't want you to focus on doing well in school. I don't want you to focus on getting the best grades or going to the best colleges. What I really want you to focus on is asking yourself how you can serve humanity and asking yourself what your unique talents are. Because you have a unique talent that no one else has, and you have a special way of expressing that talent, and no one else has it." His children ended up going to the best schools, getting the best grades. They are financially self-sufficient because they are focused on what they are here to give.

Rabbi Shmuley Boteach, who counsels families in crisis and is seen on The Learning Channel's *Shalom in the Home,* said on *The Oprah Winfrey Show,* "We parents believe that if we take the hammer and chisel, we can sculpt our children into an image of what we want them to be. When it is so much more effective to get them to hear their own inner voice of what they want to be."

How do you esteem your child? Do you really honor who he or she is? Do you light up when your child enters the room? Remember a time when someone you know was really excited to see you. It was a great feeling was it not? My grandchildren light up when they see me. It makes me feel loved and lovable. Do not become so accustomed to your child that you treat him or her like the furniture . . . just there. Or worse, we see them and immediately remind them of what we want them to do: *Wipe your feet. Do your homework. Wash the dishes. Clean your room.* The next time they enter the room, try lighting up. See how they respond.

Unconditional Love

Nothing will cause your child to esteem himself more than your unconditional love for him. He must feel that no matter what he does or does not do, he is loved without conditions, and that he is loved just because he exists. What are the conditions you unconsciously put on your love for your child?

I did Rapid Eye sessions with a man who was having anxiety attacks. These attacks went away when he remembered being ten years old and participating in a boxing competition. He felt pressure from the adults in his life to perform well. The emotions he had that day in the boxing ring were the same he was feeling now which preceded his panic attacks: worry, scared, do not want to lose, fear of failure, and letting others down. Whether his parents put too much pressure on him to win or he created that in his own mind, reassuring words from them, that win or lose they loved him and esteemed him because he exists and because he is their son, could have helped him to relax and enjoy his activity without the stress.

I always felt loved as a child. I know now that my parents loved me unconditionally, but at the time I had a lot of fear that it was conditional because of the following experience. On my fourteenth birthday my parents took me aside and gave me an expensive coat. It was a white furry coat that was very stylish at that time. They said, "We want you to know how much we love you. We can't do this for your siblings, but we just wanted you to know we appreciate you because you always do everything you are supposed to do." I appreciated my parents for giving me the coat, but I remember thinking that this must mean that they did not love my siblings because they did not do what my parents thought they should. And I had better be perfect, or I would not be loved. I remember feeling so much pressure to be good. I either had to be perfect, or I had to hide my errors. I know now it was not what they really meant, but in my young mind, I was afraid of making a mistake and being unloved. I spent a lot of years with this misperception.

They're Singing Your Song
From *A Path With Heart* by Jack Cornfield

"When a woman in a certain African tribe knows she is pregnant, she goes out into the wilderness with a few friends and together they pray and meditate until they hear the song of the child. They recognize that every soul has its own vibration that expresses its unique flavor and purpose. When the women attune to the song, they sing it out loud. Then they return to the tribe and teach it to everyone else.

When the child is born, the community gathers and sings the child's song to him or her. Later, when the child enters education, the village gathers and chants the child's song. When the child passes through the initiation to adulthood, the people again come together and sing. At the time of marriage, the person hears his or her song. Finally, when the soul is about to pass from this world, the family and friends gather at the person's bed, just as they did at their birth, and they sing the person to the next life.

A friend is someone who knows your song and sings it to you when you have forgotten it. Those who love you are not fooled by mistakes you have made or dark images you hold about yourself. They remember your beauty when you feel ugly; your wholeness when you feel broken; your innocence when you feel guilty; and your purpose when you are confused.

You may not have grown up in an African tribe that sings your song to you at crucial life transitions, but life is always reminding you when you are in tune with yourself and when you are not. When you feel good, what you are doing matches your song, and when you feel awful, it doesn't. In the end, we shall all recognize our song and sing it well. You may feel a little warble at the moment, but so have all the great singers. Just keep singing and you'll find your way home."

This beautiful story can inspire us to help our children to be his or her true authentic self. Help them to remember who they really are, and that it is not what they do. Help them to know their uniqueness, their beauty, their wholeness, and that they have a purpose. Let them know that your love for them has no conditions so that they can love themselves unconditionally. Remind them that they are not broken. Let them know that whether they hit a home run, or strike out, or sit in a wheel chair with no use of their arms or legs, that they are loved and lovable just because they exist. Sing them their song until they can sing it themselves.

Forgiveness

A middle-aged man came to me for help. He wanted to forgive his ex-wife but found it very difficult. He said he knew he should forgive her but just could not do it. In the Rapid Eye session we got to the root of the problem. He had not forgiven himself for things he perceived as wrong and unforgivable. At sixteen he had accidentally burned his house down. At nineteen he had gotten a girl pregnant. His belief that these two events made him unforgivable stood in the way of him being able to forgive himself . . . and his ex-wife. Once he changed his belief that *all* things are forgivable and that *he* is deserving of forgiveness, he forgave himself *and* his ex-wife. It was a huge relief to give up this burden that he had carried for many years.

We must forgive ourselves before we can forgive others. Guilt holds us back. It stagnates us. How do we teach our children the powerful healing lesson of forgiveness? Like everything else. By example. By letting them see us forgive. By forgiving them. By letting them know that there are no mistakes, just lessons to learn. By non-judgement.

Exercises
For Creating New Parenting Patterns

1. Journal ways you see that you are trying to mold your child into something you want them to be. Then journal how you can change your focus on helping them to be who they are.

2. Consider writing a song just for your child. (You could use the tune of any song you choose and just write your own lyrics.) If your child is older, they could help or even do it themselves.

3. Practice forgiving yourself and others. Journal your experiences.

4. Find a way to express to your child "I love who you are, just the way you are. You don't have to BE anything other than who you are right now. You are loved and lovable."

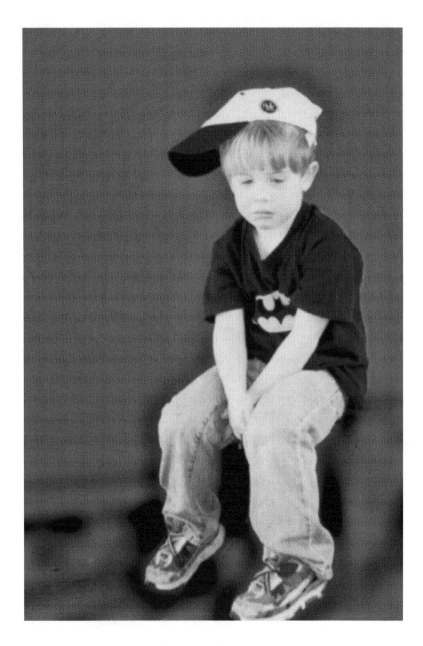

Anything we do over and over becomes a pattern.
It becomes so natural that we do it without thinking.

Chapter 8
Why Children Do What They Do

Birth and Before

B irth is our first impression of life. It is well known that a traumatic experience can have a huge effect on a person's life, and birth is a very traumatic event. Although we do not consciously remember our birth and before, it is in our subconscious. The imprint of our birth is recorded in every cell of our body. Birth memories have emerged through practices such as hypnosis, psychoanalysis, deep breathing techniques, and in Rapid Eye Therapy. Some of the best information on birth and how it affects us is in David Chamberlain's *The Mind of Your Newborn Baby*.

The Rapid Eye model teaches that most issues go back to our birth. That is why we usually begin with birth work in a RET session. (See diagram on page 90.)

A young woman of average weight came in for Rapid Eye sessions. Her presenting issue was that she was consumed with the constant thought that she needed to be just a little smaller. She said she knew she was a normal size, but she could hardly think of anything else. Through the Rapid Eye process I took her back in time to her birth and before. See the diagram on the next page for the sequence we use for this.

She had a very long birth, so she was in the birth canal a long time. As she experienced the memory of being in the birth canal, I asked her how she felt. She said, "I feel

(Compliments of the Rapid Eye Institute)

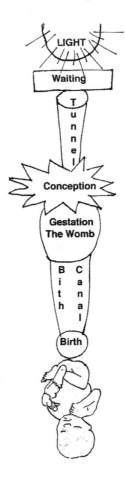

like if I was just a little smaller I could get out of here." Bingo. Her eyes popped open as if a light bulb had come on.

We were able to release the emotion of the first time she felt she needed to be a little smaller and change that old belief and pattern that had begun in the birth canal.

Many people do not know why they do not feel more connected to God. Often they even feel unloved by God. We left the warm loving feeling we had in the light to come to earth. The pain of leaving God can cause us to feel unloved and separate from Him. During a Rapid Eye session many people feel the love of God for the first time in their life. The love was always there, but now they can feel it.

In the womb the baby feels every emotion the mother feels. If the mother has a traumatic experience, such as the death of a parent, divorce, or financial worries, the baby will feel her grief, sadness, or worry. The baby may interpret those feelings as "Mom is sad she is pregnant," "I'm the cause of the divorce," or "I'm too much trouble."

Think of how traumatic it is to leave the light (God) and then how it must feel to be "kicked out" of the womb into an ultra bright, loud, and cold world. We are then poked, prodded, and laughed at. Little boys are circumcised—what could be more traumatic, and little girls are examined in a way that sometimes leaves them feeling sexually abused. Many women tell me they have the feeling of having been sexually abused but do not think they were. The examination at birth can cause this feeling.

After birth, many babies are taken away from their mother for extended periods of time, leaving the baby with feelings of "Women are never there for me," "I'm all alone," or "I've been abandoned."

One man I worked with had many emotional issues that seemed to center around feeling unloved. He acknowledged having a functional, loving family, but he felt his mother did not love him. In doing emotional work on his birth, he remembered feeling unloved during the ninth month of his mother's pregnancy. He cleared the feeling and got a sense that his mother did indeed love him but wondered what his mother was experiencing during this time. After the session he contacted his mother. She could not remember anything unusual happening, but she went to her journal and found an entry of just before he was born when something happened that caused her to feel unloved by her husband. He had taken on his mother's feeling of being unloved.

Childhood Trauma

We have all had trauma in our lives growing up. Sometimes it is big things like abuse, death of a loved one, or the divorce of parents. Sometimes it is small, seemingly inconsequential things, but in the mind of a child it can have a lasting effect. Some of the traumas are remembered vividly, and some are suppressed.

A woman came to me saying she dreaded Christmas because she always got sick. With RET she remembered a time when she was thirteen that her father was out of work and a church or school group brought gifts for the family. Her mother refused the gifts with the remark, "We are fine. We don't need the gifts." From the thirteen-year-old's perspective, not only were they too poor for Christmas, but she was not even deserving of a gift. This long-forgotten memory was the cause of her unconsciously disliking Christmas so much that she avoided it by becoming sick each year.

Another young woman came to see me who was pursuing a singing career. She felt she was blocking herself from success. She went back to a time at age twelve when her dad laughed at her and said, "You can't do that. You need to do something better with your life." She was able to forgive her dad for his careless remark and change her belief that "I can't do that" and "I'm not doing anything good with my life." Some time later I got a letter saying,

"There has been a difference in my life since my sessions with you. My prayer life is better, and I meditate longer and can stay focused now. My vocal manager and producer has been blown away at the difference in my singing."

A man who has experienced much success in life, in most areas, was not so successful in his relationships. He had been through two or three divorces, and his current relationship was rocky. He said it seemed as if he experiences the same types of problems over and over and always ends up with women who do not make him happy. "I do everything I can to make them happy, but I don't get what I need from the relationship." He had underlying beliefs of "I am unworthy of love," "love is painful," and "women can't give me what I want." He was raised by a single mom and grandmother, and in our Rapid Eye session he recalled a time when he was three years old. He remembered asking them for something that they could not provide for him. He saw himself pout when he did not get what he wanted. The light bulb came on when he saw this, and he said, "My girlfriend told me at lunch today that I was pouting like a three year old!" The experience of being told no may not seem like a big deal.

We have all experienced that. But for him it started a pattern of troubled relationships, not because his mom said no, but because of how he *perceived* it.

These patterns become stronger with time as we recreate it over and over. Our subconscious mind will look for instances in our life to prove to ourselves that "women can't give me what I want" or whatever the case may be. When we see the first event with understanding, we can now consciously create something different. To create a healthy and satisfying relationship or anything else we want, we must become conscious and aware and create our life from the present instead of from our childhood. If we create from our childhood, we will be acting out the same pattern time after time, giving us more of what we do not want.

Creating Patterns

Anything that we do over and over becomes a pattern. Every pattern has a beginning, and every time we do the behavior, it feels more and more natural. In fact, it becomes so natural that we do it without thinking. Remember the first time you got on a bicycle? It was probably very difficult and took a lot of effort and conscious thought. You had to balance, move your feet, hold on with your hands, and watch where you were going all at the same time. The next time you got on, it was the same only a little easier, until finally you could get on and ride without falling. Given enough experience on the bicycle you could eventually ride the bike and enjoy it. It is now easy, and you can ride effortlessly.

Many patterns serve us well. Riding a bike is one. Tying your shoes, brushing your teeth, and bathing are all patterns that serve us well. Other patterns we develop do not serve us so well. The man who develops a pattern of pouting when he does not get what he wants in relationships with women, is no longer served well by that pattern. The person who turns to alcohol or drugs to numb his feelings is no longer served by the pattern of addiction because he is now controlled by the drugs and has not dealt with his issues but just covered them up with numbness and denial.

Every pattern in our life has a beginning, a first time we behaved in that specific way. It can begin with something happening. Then we have a feeling about it. Then we develop a belief about it. We then behave in a certain way. The following example shows how this is created:

A young child is the oldest of three. He's very bright and is given the typical love and affection a child gets in a family environment. His younger siblings are also bright and cute, and, perhaps because they are younger, they get lots of attention. They are told "how cute and adorable" they are. Maybe the attention is actually equally distributed, but in the oldest child's mind he gets less attention. It does not really matter if it is real or perceived, but if he *thinks* the attention is less, that is his reality—that he gets less attention. This is the beginning of a pattern.

1. An event happens (real or imagined): He gets less attention than his siblings.
2. We have a feeling about it: "I feel unloved."
3. We develop a belief about it: "I must be unlovable."
4. We behave in a certain way: He is mean to siblings and parents, acting unlovable.

As time goes on, the behavior of being mean and behaving in an *unlovable* way creates others treating him in an unlovable way.

He then thinks, "See. I knew I was unlovable." He continues this cycle and keeps finding evidence that he is unlovable. Then a really big event happens; his parents divorce, and Dad moves out. Now he really feels unlovable, thinking, "Dad doesn't love me because I'm unlovable, and he doesn't want to stay here any more." His mean and unlovable behavior intensifies because in his mind he is the problem. As he carries this pattern into teen-hood and adulthood, it increasingly becomes a part of an unhappy and dysfunctional life.

Even physical problems can often be eliminated when we go back to the first time we experienced it. Such was the case of a woman with a tightness in her chest. No physical problems were found by her doctor. She wondered if it had an emotional cause, and she remembered a time at age ten when she had been thrown down and had the breath knocked out of her. When she let go of the emotions surrounding this trauma, she no longer experienced the discomfort in her chest.

A woman came to me because she had intense fear of others being angry with her. She was miserable at work because she was so afraid that she would do something that her boss or co-workers would become angry about. She had a hard time in relationships because she spent all her time and energy trying to please her partner so that he would not become angry with her. In every situation she was unhappy because she was afraid of others becoming angry. In the session she was asked to go back in time to the first event that she felt afraid of someone becoming angry. She remembered a time when she was six years old and her mother becoming angry and abusive with her, and she did not know what she had done to invoke her mother's wrath. That was the beginning of a pattern that continued into adulthood. The pattern showed up in every area of her life. Realizing this, she was now free to begin to let go of this pattern that was making her life miserable, and can now choose to create a new pattern that will bring her freedom and joy.

Even if you have repeated a pattern for many years, you can change the pattern and create a new one in its place. Understanding how it started and letting it go is the first step. Creating something new by consciously choosing a new way is the next step. And every time you do it a new way, just like every time you get on that bicycle, it gets easier and easier until the new way becomes the new pattern, a pattern that serves you well, bringing you freedom and joy instead of fear and disfunction. If life is lived unconsciously, it will be like living the same movie over and over again, only with different actors.

DNA or Past Life

Many people have retrieved memories, through RET, hypnosis, or other means. These memories that are recorded in our cells, can be DNA memories from our ancestors, or from past lives. Many people have strong opinions about the reality of past lives. Some strongly believe and others strongly disbelieve. There is also the possibility that our mind creates a story around the issues we are experiencing. The truth is we do not know, but in retrieving these memories healing often occurs. If the subconscious mind takes us to a memory that is not from our lifetime, then it is significant for us in some way. If the practitioners suggestion is to "go to the first time this pattern was created" and the client sees someone of a different sex, in a different time, and in a location different from the one he or she has ever lived, we must consider the possibility of a past-life memory or a DNA memory. As a Rapid Eye technician, my intention is not to prove or disprove the reality of these memories, but rather to assist my client to heal and move forward to a happier and more functional life. Regardless of the origin of these memories, they do exist, and many are healed from the disfunction in their lives by recalling these memories.

Exercises
For Creating New Parenting Patterns

1. If your mother is still living, find out the details of your birth.

2. Recall the details of your child's birth. Share with them what a glorious day it was and how glad you are they were born.

3. What are five or so events in your life that had lasting effects on you? Pick one of them and journal the four steps explained in this chapter under "Creating a Pattern."

We all respond to love. We thrive on it. It heals us.

CHAPTER 9
Children of Divorce & Other Difficult Situations

The Miracle Dog

A couple of years ago a stray dog showed up at my daughter LeAnne's apartment. Dana was sick, underweight, and had a bad case of the mange and fleas. She had a deformed hip, a crippled leg, and was pregnant. She was in terrible shape, the worst I had ever seen. Dana was immediately protective of my daughter who lived alone and wanted a dog to keep her company and to help her feel safe. In spite of the dog's poor condition, she seemed happy.

A trip to the veterinarian did not help Dana. LeAnne began to "doctor" Dana herself as well as feed and care for her. Family, friends, and neighbors all loved and cared for Dana. Even those who were not fond of animals seemed to love her. Within a few short months, Dana became a healthy dog. She lost the puppy she was carrying but has gone on to give birth to two litters of beautiful, healthy puppies. She still limps from the crippled leg and hip, but today, five years later, she continues to be healthy and happy, and she is a wonderful companion.

I call Dana The Miracle Dog. To me she represents all of us, all of humankind. If Dana could talk, I am sure she would have an interesting story to tell—one of abuse, abandonment, and being unwanted and neglected. But that is only part of her story. The rest of the story is one of hope, unconditional love and giving. We all respond to love. We thrive on it. It heals us. She received love, and I believe that love healed her. She also gave love, and that is what heals us.

In my private practice, I see people who in many ways are like Dana. Many have been abused or neglected. Others feel abandoned and unwanted. Some have experienced unspeakable things. We *all* have wounds of one kind or another.

Beating the Odds

Children who experience their parents divorcing have been said to be at a disadvantage over children whose parents stay together. In the United States, more than half of all children experience their parents divorcing, and 40 percent of children are raised without fathers. Children of divorce are more likely to be physically unhealthy, receive lower grades in school, need psychological help, drop out of high school, become a pregnant teen, abuse drugs, and experience divorce in their own marriage. These statistics can be very distressing. These statistics are precisely why we must address the issues of the 50 percent of children who experience divorce.

I once heard a young mother say, "I know my kids are going to have lots of problems because their dad left us." I cringed when she said it. If that is her belief, she will help create that. Even though there is a chance for children of divorce to experience problems, there is also a chance for them to experience health, success and happiness. Look at this child as you would any other. Look at them as whole and perfect and brimming with wonderful possibilities for health and happiness.

Many of the great people of the world have come from disfunction or hardship. Oprah Winfrey was born in rural Mississippi to black unwed parents. She was raised by her grandmother, then her mother, and finally her father. She was sexually abused at a young age and became pregnant at the age of fourteen. No need to expound on her success, but she is one of the richest and most successful people in America. Her contribution to the world is astounding. Thomas Edison was considered stupid and unteachable and had only three months of formal education. At the age of six he was publicly whipped by his father for burning down his family's barn. He had to go to work at age twelve. Wayne Dyer's childhood years were difficult. His father walked away from the family, and much of Dyer's childhood and teenage years were spent in orphanages and foster homes. In spite of this, he received his doctorate in counseling psychology and is an inspiring author and motivational speaker. He created great wealth in his life and gave it all away, only to create it all again.

There are many people, some famous and some not, who come from less-than-perfect circumstances. I had a client who along with her two sisters was beaten by her mother every day from the time she was eight years old. Her childhood was totally dysfunctional. Her father died at age eight and her stepfather committed suicide. She experienced the death of many other people in her life, including giving birth to a stillborn child. But she chose to create a different experience for herself and her children. She married a man who was good to her and their children. She developed a good relationship with her own children and never abused them. With love and compassion, she reaches out to children and families in domestic violence with her work with abuse shelters, state reformatories, mental health centers, and public schools. She says she had a choice to come through these experiences *better* or *bitter.* She chose better.

Look at the people around you. They all have a story to tell. *You* have a story to tell. We all have dysfunction, hardship, or difficulties of some type. Do not write anyone off—your child, your self . . . not anyone. If a child experiences divorce, it is just that—an experience. Follow the lead of other great men and women who have used their life experiences to become healthy, happy, contributing human beings.

If you are divorced and worry about your child, start by letting them know you believe in them. Love them and see in them not dysfunction, but a perfect spirit being having a human experience. Let us do our best to provide the best possible environment for our children. There is no question that children thrive in a healthy two-parent home. Every effort to give them that should be taken. But if that is not possible, do not compound the problem by assuming dysfunction is inevitable.

Many people fear that if we downplay the negative effects of divorce or offer help for families who are experiencing a breakup, we are encouraging divorce. This is no more true than thinking that by addressing sexual abuse and helping people who have experienced it, we are encouraging sexual abuse. Help for 50 percent of our population is overdue. Divorced parents who are groping in the dark for a way to help their hurting children want the same thing that the other half of the population want, a way to help their child overcome whatever stands in the way of that child's happiness.

Understanding and help is here. Gary Neuman is the creator of the Sandcastles Therapy Program, a nationwide divorce therapy program for children. This program was first instituted in Miami, Florida, and it is now mandatory there and elsewhere for minor children whose parents are filing for divorce. His website is www. mgaryneuman.com, and his book is *Helping Your Kids Cope with Divorce*. His help for children and parents experiencing divorce is the best I have seen.

I believe that the three greatest fears and concerns that children experience when their parents divorce are as follows:

1. "The Divorce Is My Fault."

Children almost always think that if they would have been better, the divorce would not have happened. Tell your child from the beginning that Mom and Dad's relationship is Mom and Dad's responsibility. Assure the child that they are not the cause of your problems. Taking full responsibility for the divorce is absolutely essential for you as well as your child. You do not have to tell them the details of the marriage problems to assure them that it is not their fault. You should not burden them with that anyway. Believing they caused the breakup of their family is too heavy of a burden for a child to bear. It is *not* their fault. You must do everything in your power to eliminate this untrue belief.

2. "If Dad Left, I could Lose Mom Too." (If Mom Left, Dad Could Leave.)

Be understanding and gentle with your child if he cries for you more than usual or if he is afraid to be out of your sight. A young child may become upset when you are in another room. He may even worry that you could die. Be patient and assure him that he will always be taken care of and that you are always coming back. Explain that even though Dad (or Mom) lives somewhere else now, that he will be able to see Dad on a regular basis and that he can call Dad whenever he wants. If this is not possible or in the best interest of the child, care should be taken to assure the child that this is not his fault, that you understand how hard it is for him not to see Dad, and that you are there for the child. It is a very scary feeling for a child to think of losing parents. Be confident and assure the child that he will be taken care of. Keep as many things constant as possible. Staying in the same school, house, and routine are helpful. Also, continuing to see the same friends and relatives (Mom's *and* Dad's) also helps to maintain a sense of stability in the otherwise unstableness of divorce.

3. "If Dad and Mom Don't Love Each Other Anymore, Maybe They Don't Love Me Anymore Either."

All any of us want is to be loved. If we feel unloved, we assume that we must be unlovable. And if we believe we are unlovable, then we think no one can love us. Divorced parents should be sensitive to this issue and give constant reassurance to the child that he is loved by *both* parents. Assure the child that you love him and that the other parent loves him and that your marriage problems have nothing to do with your love for your child. If you can find it in your heart to feel any love for your ex-spouse, I believe it is helpful to tell the child that even if you cannot be together as husband and wife, you still love each other. Love, after all, is unconditional. This can help assure the child that they too are loved unconditionally.

One young girl in a session with me whose parents were divorcing told me she was happy. "Don't get me wrong," she said. "I'm *not* happy about my parents divorcing, but I *am* happy Mom and Dad and lots of other people love me, and that Mom and Dad still love each other." Feeling loved is what will get this child through this difficult experience of divorce.

Your child needs *lots* of reassurance that he is loved, that it is not his fault, and that he will be taken care of. The following positive affirmations are some of what I have used with children experiencing divorce or turmoil in the home. You can say these to the child. Having the child repeat them after you can be powerful as well. If they will not do this, it also works well to say the affirmations to your child after he is asleep. Be sure he is in REM sleep (their eyes will flutter under their eyelids). Feel free to add some of your own or change any you feel impressed to change. (Use "I am" or "you are" depending on how you use them.) Say these or similar ones often. None of us hear enough positive. All children need to hear these, especially through the experience of divorce.

- Mom and Dad's problems are Mom and Dad's problems.
- I am *not* the cause of their problems.
- It is not my fault.
- It is okay to feel sad about their problems.
- It is okay to feel mad about their problems.
- I choose *now* to let go of thinking and feeling that their problems are my fault.
- Since their problems belong to them, I now know that I don't have to fix their problems. That is not my job.

- My job is to (this could be something like "be a kid and have fun," or "do your best at school," or "learn to play the piano.")
- I am free to be me.
- I am a child of God.
- I am always taken care of.
- I am loved.
- I am lovable.
- Mom loves me.
- Dad loves me.
- I have *lots* of people in my life who love me (name them: Grandma, the dog, Aunt Sue . . .)
- I love me.
- I am lovable.
- I am free to look forward to the future.

Expressing Emotions

It is most important to allow and encourage your child to express what they are feeling about the divorce, about Mom, and about Dad. Do not take it personal if they express anger toward you or blame you. Just let them express how they feel. This cannot be done just once. It must be an ongoing conversation. You may have a tendency to get past the worst of it and then not to address it again. After all, it is painful for you too, but follow your divine inner guidance on how and when to do this. The *worst* thing the child can do is suppress those feelings, to stuff them deep inside. The *best* thing you can do for them is to allow them to express their feelings in the loving presence of an understanding and accepting parent.

Get Help

I highly recommend Mr. Neuman's book, *Helping Your Kids Cope With Divorce.* I think it will give you and your child much-needed help during this difficult time. If you feel the need for additional help, find a Rapid Eye technician in your area. Children do very well with RET. You will probably want to do some sessions also.

Don't let the stress of divorce impair the chances of a happy life for you and your child. Let the story you and your child tell be like that of Dana. Not the story of divorce, sadness, and dysfunction, but one of beating the odds, of hope, unconditional love, happiness, and healing.

Exercises
For Creating New Parenting Patterns

1.   Find people in your life who are like Dana, the miracle dog. Notice and journal how you now see them.

2.   Find the miracles in your own life. Journal these miracles. Notice how your perception of yourself shifts.

3.   If your parents divorced, journal your hurts. Then journal a new more powerful belief that you are not your experience.

4.   List the negative experiences your child has experienced (divorce, handicap). Now list the blessings: the ones they have in spite of these experiences and the ones they have because of the experiences. Have a conversation with your child about how you are both going to create wonderful things in your lives.

5.   Tell your child the story of Dana, the miracle dog, and discuss it with them. Listen to their insights about it.

*Enjoy the being who is in a child's body. Look to
the essence of who he or she really is and connect, not
parent to child, but spirit being to spirit being.*

CHAPTER 10
The Role of Parent

"The child has a deep longing for the parent to be there as a human being, not as a role, no matter how conscientiously that role is being played." (Elkhart Tolle, *A New Earth*) Step out of the role of parenthood. You can still function as a parent, but if you can step out of the ego's role of parenthood and just be an authentic human being, you will be able to give your child the right kind of attention. Children, like all of us, want to be loved. To a child the right kind of attention, equals love. The wrong kind of attention ("Do this. Don't do that.") causes the child to have unconscious resentment toward the parent. The child will want to know "Why don't you recognize the real me?" Just let the walls down and be yourself and let your child be his or herself. Enjoy the being who is in a child's body. Look to the essence of who he or she really is and connect, not parent to child, but spirit being to spirit being. You are not superior. Your child is not inferior. You are here together as equals having this earthly experience.

Many times parents just want to look good and feel good as a parent. If this is the case, we are using the child for our own ego gratification. This is a form of exploitation. If a parent's purpose for putting their child in an activity, that could otherwise be fun and worthwhile for the child, is not for the benefit of the child, it will be an ego trip for the parent. A child needs to experience life free from feelings of having to feed the parents' ego.

Example

Example is the best teacher. The old adage "Do as I say, not as I do" is what we would like to be able to work for us, but it does not. Children will do what you do. Refer back to chapter 6 about mirrors. What we see them do is only what we have done.

Having All the Answers

My son-in-law tells the story of being in a confrontation with his dad when he was a teen. They had a difference of opinion as teens and parents sometimes do. His dad said to him, "Hey, I don't have all the answers, and I've never been the dad of a teen before." This admission took the teen by surprise. It had a huge impact on him and helped him become the good and understanding man he is today. I believe it is so important to have this perspective as a parent. We do not know everything the instant our child is born. Even us "seasoned parents" do not know everything. We are learning and gaining experience as we go, just as the child is. The presumption that we are all-knowing is piousness.

Before You Become a Mom

My father always had this saying for me and my sisters as we were growing up: "Before you become somebody's wife or parent, become somebody." I passed it along to my own children.

Although I see things differently now and believe we do not have to *become* anything, this statement still has merit if looked at a little differently.

Gaining more life experience before you enter the long-term commitment of marriage and parenting is a very good thing. Also developing interests and hobbies or involving yourself in causes and pursuits you enjoy and have passion for can help you bring more to the "table" of your relationships with your spouse and children. Although some of these interests may have to be put on hold at times during your child's childhood, they can be a source of continued enjoyment, giving you an interest other than your child's life, and creating balance and added fulfillment to your life. This is especially important for stay-at-home moms.

You can get so caught up in parenting that you will forget to take care of yourself. If you do not take care of you, you cannot take care of your child. Nourishing yourself with what you love to do creates balance and joy. A joyful man or woman does not have to *try* to be a good parent. To a joyful woman, being a mother will come more naturally. Many women get so caught up in trying to be the very best parent that they lose the joy of it. They often live their lives *for* their child when they should be living their lives *with* their child. The same is true in the marriage relationship. Living your life *for* your partner denotes inequality and causes unhappiness. Living your life *with* your partner suggests equality and happiness and creates a fulfilling and joyful life. You must be *you* in any relationship. You must be the real, authentic, true you. You can give up a lot of things as a parent or a partner, but you cannot give up yourself. You must be true to you. When you are your true, authentic, real, and awesome self, parenthood will flow more naturally and easily, and your child will thrive. He or she will follow your lead in being his or her true, authentic, real, and awesome self.

Fostering Independence

It is widely know that a common interest or hobby can bring unity and fulfillment to a family. Family fun with camping, swimming, hiking, or whatever you choose creates a bond that lasts a lifetime. It is also important to allow and even encourage your child, especially your teen, to pursue their own interest, even if you do not enjoy it or know anything about it. My own children excelled in things their mom or dad knew little about, and it was fulfilling to me as a parent to have them teach me more about their interests. It was also a source of enjoyment to watch them develop in their pursuits. Give them lots of opportunities to try out a variety of things, and they will best know their own likes and dislikes.

It Takes a Village

Many have asked if it is possible to raise a child without a church. Community is important for children and us as well. In fact, we cannot escape being part of a community. To isolate ourselves from others is to deny our sociality as well as an important resource to help children learn how to get along. As discussed in chapter 1, a church can provide a community and social network that can be of great benefit to you and your family. However, never let a church or any other organization take over the raising of your child. Be satisfied that the church meets your criteria for a healthy community, including teaching from a place of love and not fear. Many look to the church to be the final authority on morality. Teach your child to have their own moral compass. Teach your child how to go within to get their own answers. Teach them to question everything. Teach them that if something does not feel right to come and talk to you about it.

Other People's Children

Our village (community, school, church, extended family) is where we and our children intermingle with others. As we cross paths with children other than our own, be mindful that this child may benefit from something you have to offer. I am very grateful for the other adults in my children's lives who have been an influence for good. Sometimes a teacher, parent of your child's friend, or another significant adult can influence in a way that you cannot. I have heard it said that it takes one human being who really cares to make a difference in a life.

Be the human being who really cares about *all* children and make a difference in their lives. Be mindful of *all* the children in the village. We may never know the effect we have.

Boundaries

Children can be such an example of unconditional love, kindness, non-judgement, and quick forgiveness. This is a wonderful thing. Follow their lead. But it is very important to teach children about boundaries and that they can say *no*, even if the person who crosses their boundaries is a parent, teacher, minister or another child. Oftentimes children are told, "Do what the teacher (parent, church leader, or other authority figure) says." The conflict comes when the authority figure is not respectful of the child and crosses personal boundaries.

The following poem could be memorized by the whole family. Learning about and establishing boundaries and living these words would eliminate most abuse and a lot of relationship problems.

> If you are big and I am small,
> I can say "yes" or "Not at all!"
> If you are small and I am huge,
> I will still have respect for you.

Like everything else we want for our children, boundaries must be learned and practiced by us first. Until we safeguard our own personal boundaries, we cannot help our child with his or her boundaries. We cannot teach what we do not understand and practice.

It is our responsibility to establish our personal boundaries. Good boundaries make for healthy relationships. Some people are respectful of our boundaries; others are not. People with no boundaries for themselves seem to be the ones who have no respect for the boundaries of others. Have you ever felt like someone has taken advantage of you? You say to yourself, "I can't believe they did that!" Sometimes we just expect them to read our minds and know where our boundaries are. If someone crosses your boundaries, it is *your* responsibility to let them know where your boundaries are and that they have crossed the line. This is very hard for some of us to do. We do not want to hurt their feelings or make them angry with us. We all want to be "nice" and not upset anyone. We have fear of what they will think of us or what they will do in return. Fear of rejection is huge for many.

A client I worked with made great strides in being able to establish boundaries and express them to others in a loving way. She told me the following experience:

My son and his wife were having marital problems. When they told me this I was of course heartbroken. I loved my daughter-in-law, and I wanted to maintain the good relationship I had established with her as well as my son, but I knew it was not wise to be "in the middle" of their relationship. She began to tell me their marital issues. This was a very uncomfortable place to be. I still loved her and wanted to be supportive and show my unconditional love, but being in the middle was not good for me or for them. I knew I had to let her know my boundaries. I explained to her that I was not willing to listen to anything about the marriage problems and my reasons why, and then I assured her that my love for her hadn't changed. I had a lot of fear about doing this, but she accepted it and said she understood. A second time she approached me and wanted to talk about their issues. I reminded her of my previously declared boundaries, and she quickly dropped it. There was no anger on her part or mine. I feel the relationship was saved, even enhanced, because of this. I must say I am proud of myself for being able to do this. It was hard at first, but like you said, every time I do it a new way, doing the new pattern becomes easier.

A young couple with a baby got in an argument. The man became physically abusive by grabbing the woman and pushing her across the room. The woman immediately let him know that physical abuse was not acceptable by telling him if he ever did that again, she would take their child and leave and he would not see them again. She meant it and he knew it. The boundary was established and was never crossed again.

On the other hand in another relationship, slowly and little by little, a woman allowed her husband to cross her personal boundaries by belittling her, controlling her, and sexually abusing her for many years. One day she decided she had had enough and tried to set the boundaries she should have set at the beginning of the relationship. Changing the boundaries after allowing this abuse to go on for so long is like building a fence after the cows have gotten into the garden and trampled and destroyed everything. You cannot be upset with the cows because you failed to build the fence. The setting of boundaries too late was the demise of the marriage. Although abuse of any kind should not be excused, we can understand that this man was never told what the boundaries were in the marriage. The longer you allow others to cross your personal boundaries, the harder it is to establish and maintain those boundaries.

Children learn about boundaries in the home. If we have our own boundaries and if we honor other people's boundaries, your child will learn this from you. Having boundaries in the home and talking about boundaries is crucial in teaching children how to have their own boundaries. If a child does not learn to establish boundaries and to respect the boundaries of others, the way is being paved for being a victim or a perpetrator.

Boundaries should be established at an early age. Some possible boundaries for *everyone* in the home (children, teens, and parents) could be as follows:

- Privacy in the bathroom. No one should have to allow a family member to come into the bathroom while they are bathing or using the toilet.
- Purses and wallets. Children should not be allowed to go through their mom's purse. Permission could be given on occasion.
- Personal items should not be used unless permission from the owner is given.
- Mail, phone conversations, journals, and email are personal and should be respected as such.

An exception to all of the above would be if the safety and well being of the child is at stake. An example would be if there is suspected drug abuse, or if internet predators are violating the child's boundaries.

Having boundaries with our children teaches them how to have their own boundaries. Although many parents say no way too much, it is important to say no when the child crosses the boundaries that we must put up to avoid becoming a slave to a disrespectful or thoughtless child. The following could be some of the personal boundaries a parent might put up for themselves:

- **Bedtime at a set time.** This is good for the child as well as a personal boundary for the parent so that you can have some time for yourself after they go to bed.
- **The parent's bedroom is off limits to the child.** This may not be possible with a baby or very small child, but as soon as possible, the child should respect the privacy of the parent's bedroom.
- **Everyone having chores**. If the child is not helping at home, the parent becomes a slave to the child.
- **No one saying disrespectful things.** Feelings and disagreements can always be expressed in a calm and respectful way.
- **No hitting.** A small child will sometimes hit a parent or another child. Let them know it is unacceptable.

Quiet Time

We live in a noisy, fast-paced world. Television, radios, iPods, computers, and sports events overstimulate us to the point of exhaustion. Even most restaurants are noisy and chaotic, making it hard to enjoy the meal and even harder to digest our food. We rush to work, school, and the gym. We dash to the grocery store, the car wash, and the little league game, and then we speed home to whip up dinner, only to gulp it down, after which we cannot remember if we ate or not. Even when we crash in front of the television, we are again overstimulated only to collapse into bed wide awake, not being able to sleep because our mind will not slow down because we are inundated with an overabundance of unwanted thoughts. If this is your life and you do not like it, consider re-evaluating and figure out how you can do it differently.

One of the most important things we can do for ourselves and our children is to have a time every day that everyone in the home is quiet. It does not have to be an hour-long meditation. It can be five minutes. Five minutes of complete quiet. Turn off the television, phones, and everything else that makes noise. Have everyone just sit and and be perfectly quiet. Pick a time that works best for the whole family. Just after supper or before bedtime works for lots of people. I start my day with meditation and prayer, but throughout the day, if things get hectic or I feel tired, I pause for just a few minutes and put it all out of my mind and just breathe. Get in the habit of doing this, and you will look forward to those quiet moments, making the hectic ones seem less stressful. Our world needs more quiet. Only we have power over our world. Embrace quiet. Be still and know God. Expose your child to quietness and God.

Instant Replay

When you feel like you did it *all wrong* in a situation with your child, do not be afraid to replay it and do it differently. "I'm sorry" and "I messed up" are words many parents are afraid to say. We do not like to admit we are wrong or that we handled a situation poorly. Sometimes when we see we handled a situation badly, we do not know how to undo it. Here are some ways to undo or redo situations.

Apologize. Do not make excuses. Just own what you did. Ask if you could do it again a different way. Example: "I am so sorry. I know how that must have hurt you. Could we just do that over?" Then have the child say or do his part over. This time you say or do it a different way. You will be amazed how this will totally erase the first incident, and it will be as if it never happened. Your child will also learn how to say "I'm sorry" and undo his or her own inappropriate behavior.

Visualize doing it differently. If your child will not accept an apology and will not replay it with you, accept that they have a right to decline the offer. Then take a few moments alone and visualize yourself doing it differently and your child responding a different way. Imagine the energy between you being loving and forgiving. I believe you will soon find that your child will become open to this type of role-playing.

Do not fall into the role of guilty parent. Hearing a parent say, "I'm a bad parent," causes the child to think, "I must be a bad child to make Mom or Dad feel like a bad parent." They now join you in your guilt. Guilt is not useful. (See chapter 13 for more on guilt.)

Re-parent. When you visualize doing anything from the past in a different way, you change the energy of it, and you change your energy. If you have a lot of guilt over things from the past, spend some time replaying it in your mind, doing it a different way. Visualize being the kind of parent you want to be, the kind of parent you are now becoming.

This technique also has been helpful for parents of teens. It is very important for a mother to show appropriate physical affection to teenage boys, and for a father to do the same with his teenage daughter. If they do not receive this, they will seek it elsewhere, perhaps in inappropriate ways. Often teens will push their parents away because they think it is not "cool" to receive affection from them. If this is the case with your child, visualize giving hugs and physical affection to them every day and visualize them lovingly receiving it from you. Before long you may experience real hugs being given and received.

"NO!"

When someone says the word "no," half of your brain does not hear it. If you say, "Do not eat that candy before dinner," half of your brain hears, "Do eat that candy before dinner." This is one reason you should eliminate, as much as possible, negative talk to your child. Another reason is that a child gives back that which he receives. If he is constantly bombarded with "no," "don't," and "stop that," his focus will be on the negative and on things he *cannot* do. He will grow up with a negative and fearful view of life. On the other hand, if positive verbal responses are received, he is more confident and less fearful. Creating a positive environment for a child can happen quite naturally when we first create it for ourselves. But in order to do that, we must first put some conscious effort into changing our negative patterns.

Notice the negative way you say things and think of a positive way to respond instead. The following are common negative phrases parents often say to children and an alternative positive way to respond.

NEGATIVE	POSITIVE
Don't mark on the wall!	Here. Draw Mommy a beautiful picture on this paper, and we'll put it on the refrigerator.
Don't eat sweets now. It'll spoil your dinner.	I'm making a great dinner. Want to save that until later?
That cake will make you fat.	This apple is really good, and it's good for you.
Don't hit your baby brother.	Give your baby brother a hug and kiss.
You can't come down until you clean your room.	I know how much you enjoy being in your room when it's clean. Would you like to do that now or do you need a little free time before you straighten it?
You can't play until you do your homework.	I was wondering if you wanted to play catch with me or your Dad after your homework is done?
You made a D in math!	Let's look at these grades. I see your English grade improved this time. Good job. Looks like you are having a little problem with math. How can I help?
No, you can't hang out at the mall with your friends. You're too young.	I'm glad you enjoy being with your friends. You have such nice and fun friends. Would you like to have them over for pizza and a movie? Maybe your little sister could spend the night with Grandma.

No one likes to be constantly criticized, said no to, or told every move to make. It does not create confident, happy children.

Internal vs. External Rewards

Constant praise of your child is certainly better than constant criticism. However, be aware that praise from you and others can create in the child a need and dependence on praise and recognition. If the child is doing things for the sole purpose of pleasing you, this can create a pattern of people pleasing or a feeling that "unless someone else sees what I do or how good I am, I'm not worth anything." We want our children to be self-motivated and self-fulfilled. We want them to enjoy their life, to be of service to others, and to be rewarded with the feeling of joy that comes from doing a good job, of helping another person, and of finding and living their purpose for being here.

I believe we can help a child create this by creating this in ourselves. We can also help them to recognize these inner feelings by commenting on their feelings or asking them how they feel.

"You did a good job on your room. I bet you enjoy being in there now."

"Wow! All A's. How does that feel?"

"I noticed you helped Mrs. Jones get her garbage can to the curb this morning. Does that feel good to help her? She's all alone now that Mr. Jones passed away."

"You really seem to enjoy your science projects. Is there anything in that area that you might want to pursue?"

"Your little brother really enjoys it when you read to him. You seemed to enjoy it as well."

This type of praise encourages him or her to go within and notice how they feel. The goal is to assist them to notice the joy within. When they begin to go within and access those feelings on their own, they will soon no longer need Mom, Dad, teachers, or anyone to validate them. The reward is not praise from anyone or anything outside of themselves. The reward is the joy within.

Exercises
For Creating New Parenting Patterns

1. Choose at least one concept from this chapter and have a conversation with your child if appropriate.

2. Choose to have an enjoyable experience with your child with the focus on the two of you as human beings instead of parent and child.

3. List your child's activities (sports, dance, etc.). After each one, answer the following questions:

    •   In what ways am I doing this for me?
    •   How does this benefit my child?
    •   How can I help this activity be more fun and worthwhile?
    •   Are there other things my child could be doing that would better benefit him or her?

4. Find at least one way you can better take care of yourself or do something that you really enjoy.

5. Make your own list of your most common negative remarks and change them to positive ones. (See examples on pages 122-123.)

6. Find an occasion you feel like you "did it all wrong" and use the appropriate technique to "replay it." (See "Instant Replay" on page 120.)

7. Find two occasions where you can help your child find the internal reward. (See examples on page 124.)

Section III
SKILLS FOR LIVING

Over the years I have taught a class called Life Skills in my community. These are in conjunction with Rapid Eye sessions and are part of the Rapid Eye program. If our old ways of doing things are not working for us, we must learn new ways to live our life. Albert Einstein has been given credit for saying, "Insanity is doing the same thing over and over again and expecting different results." The following seven basic principles are important to help us stop the insanity of old patterns that no longer serve our highest good. Teaching these principles to our children as well as living them ourselves will create a more conscious life for us all.

Many thanks to Dr. Ranae Johnson, founder of Rapid Eye Technology, for developing the Skills for Life information. Much of the information in the following seven chapters come from the manuals she created.

*Whether you think you can or you think you
can't, you're right.* (Henry Ford)

CHAPTER 11
Thought

"For as he thinketh in his heart, so is he." Proverbs 23:7. This wise statement given thousands of years ago is still relevant today. Everything starts with a thought. The account in Genesis of the creation of the earth states, "And God said, let there be light: and there was light." Our thoughts and our words are creative.

Japanese Dr. Masaru Emoto, using high-speed photography, discovered that frozen water crystals were formed revealing changes when specific thoughts were directed toward them. Water exposed to words such as "love" and "thank you" created beautiful, complex, and colorful snowflake patterns. Water exposed to negative words like "you fool" and "you make me sick" formed incomplete, asymmetrical patterns with dull colors. Considering that the body is made up of 60 to 70 percent water, this really makes one think.

Your thoughts and beliefs become your reality. You are quite literally always right! If you want to change your life, then change your thoughts. If you put food into your body that is not healthy, you will become unhealthy. Your brain works the same way. If you choose negative or toxic thoughts, those thoughts will manifest in poor choices, bad relationships, a negative attitude, an unfulfilled life, and dis-ease in the body. Henry Ford said, "Whether you think you can or you think you can't, you're right."

Scientists are now able to measure changes in immune cells and the brain to give us objective scientific proof that our thoughts create our reality. If you imagine laying on the beach in the warm sun, your blood vessels dilate, and your hands become warm just as though you were really there. A basketball player can imagine making the perfect basket, and the same neurons will fire up that do so when actually ringing that basket. Someone who believes he is being touched by a red-hot object often will produce a burn blister, even when the object was room temperature. There is growing clinical evidence that imagery is helpful in treating physical dis-ease and pain. The mind is a very powerful tool.

Limiting Beliefs vs. Empowering Beliefs

In 1954 no one believed that it was possible to run a mile in less than four minutes. No one, that is, except Roger Bannister. He ran the race, and his time was just under four minutes. The interesting thing is that once he broke the record, runners everywhere began to run the mile under four minutes also. It was as though everyone now had permission to run the mile in less than four minutes. Runners now believed it could be done. "The thing always happens that you really believe in; and the belief in a thing makes it happen." (Frank Lloyd Wright)

A limiting belief is a belief that limits what we do. It limits our possibilities. Some limiting beliefs we have as a society or as individuals are:

- Life is hard and then you die.
- No pain. No gain.
- When you turn 40, you need glasses.
- When you get old, you become sick and useless.
- I am poor. I will never have anything.
- I am a failure.
- I cannot do that.
- I cannot lose weight.
- I am a diabetic. I will always be a diabetic.
- I am depressed. There is no way out.

Our children can develop limiting beliefs based on their experiences, what we believe about them, and what we say to them. Some of their limiting beliefs could be:

- Children are to be seen and not heard.
- Teenagers cannot be trusted.
- I cannot do anything right.
- I am not smart.
- I am not pretty.
- I have to be perfect to be loved.
- If I make a mistake, I will get in trouble.

Gerold Jampolsky tells the following story in the preface of his 25th anniversary edition of his book *Love is Letting Go of Fear.*

> Dyslexic since childhood, I entered the University of California at Berkeley in 1943 knowing that a "dumbbell" English course was in my future. I struggled through it and received a D, and on the final day of class my professor

said to me, "Jampolsky, I don't know what you're going to do in life, but for God's sake, don't ever try to write a book." I was 50 years old before I decided to no longer give my power away to other people's judgements about my limitations and do what I had been told was impossible and write a book.

Jampolsky's book *Love is Letting Go of Fear* has sold over four million copies and has changed the lives of countless people. He held a limiting belief about his ability to write a book based on his teacher's comment, but once he changed that belief, a wonderful book was born. We give birth to whatever we believe.

We can help our children create empowering beliefs. Here are some empowering beliefs we could create for ourselves and our children:

- My life is fun, and I can do anything I choose.
- As I get older, I get better and better.
- I attract money, happiness, and love.
- I am loved no matter what.
- I learn from my mistakes. They are just experiences to help me grow and learn.

Be very cautious about what you say in front of your babies and children. Remember from chapter 8 that children understand everything that is said. I notice babies in their strollers or carriers among a group of women who are having conversations that they do not think their babies understand. Think again about what you say to babies. "You are so beautiful" will usually get a smile.

A negative remark will get a sad puckered up face. That pucker is *not* gas.

Poor Me

"Poor me. Look what *they* did to me. I am a failure (or unhappy) because of *them*." We blame our parents, spouses, anyone who "did us wrong." Choosing to be a victim does not really let us off the hook. It is just an excuse to be stuck. Many of us would rather be right than be happy. Remember Dana, the miracle dog in chapter 9. Dana is a very happy dog.

A woman came to me and asked me to work with her twelve-year-old son. He had much resentment toward his father who had left the family because of a divorce. I turned to the boy and acknowledged that he got a "bum deal" because no twelve-year-old boy deserves to have his father leave. If he would be willing to try to forgive his father so that he could have some peace about it and be happy again, I would be glad to help. He looked me right in the eyes and said, "Not until I am eighteen." He would rather be right than happy, at least for a while. If he stays unhappy and bitter about his dad, he can say, "See what my dad did to me." He wanted to play the victim, as many of us do. Victims become stuck in misery and will stay stuck until they choose to take full responsibility for their lives. We cannot control others' choices, but we can control how we respond to them and how we choose to let it affect us.

The following are some examples of how to rephrase our negative thoughts. The goal is to honor our feelings and emotions, then let the negative ones go and choose a new thought and feeling, creating a new reality.

Negative Thought	Positive Rephrase
I am angry.	I feel angry.
I am sad and lonely.	I now choose _____.
You make me so mad!	I am noticing that I feel upset with you.
I hate myself.	I trade in my self hatred for I am accepting myself just as I am.
I am such a loser.	Even though I sometimes feel like a loser, I love myself, and I am okay.
I am getting sick.	I feel sick. I choose health now.

Helpful hints:

- Say "I *feel* (negative emotion)" instead of "I *am* (negative emotion)." Acknowledging your emotion is healthy, but saying "I am" is a powerful way to become the negative emotion.

- "I am just noticing that _____" is a way to acknowledge your negative emotion or an unpleasant situation. It is a way to step back and be the observer.

- "I now choose (pick what you would rather feel)." This puts your focus on the positive so that you create feeling positive instead negative. It *is* a choice.

- "I trade in my (negative feeling) for (positive feeling)."

- "Even though I feel (negative feeling), I love myself, and I am okay (or safe)." Acceptance of ourselves and our feelings is essential to being happy and creating positive change.

Here are some examples of how to change your limiting beliefs into empowering beliefs:

Limiting Belief	Empowering Belief
No pain, no gain.	Every time I (work out, run) it gets easier and easier.
Life is hard and then you die.	I come through life's challenges victorious and happy.
I am such a failure. I'll never amount to anything.	I am successful because every time I fall, I get back up. Each time I get up, I learn something that helps me to be a better person.
It's my parents' fault. They divorced when I was young.	I forgive my parents. They did the best they knew how. I am free to choose something different for my life.
I can't change. I'm just like Dad (Mom).	I am choosing change. I am living my own life.

An amazing story of someone who used their positive thoughts and empowering beliefs to create a miracle is Morris Goodman. He was 35 years old and highly successful when the airplane he was piloting crashed. He was so severely injured that all he could do was blink his eyes. He could not breathe, eat, or perform any bodily functions on his own. His neck was broken, his spinal cord crushed, and every major muscle in his body destroyed. Doctors told him that if he survived he would be a vegetable. He did not believe the doctors and chose instead to create something different. With his positive thoughts, empowering beliefs, and visualizations he walked out of the hospital on his own by Christmas, which was his goal. This is why he is referred to as "The Miracle Man." You can find his story at www.themiracleman.org.

It seems like such a simple thing to think our way to happiness. Like most things, it takes conscious effort until it becomes a new habit or pattern. Every time you do it differently, every time you change your negative thought to a positive one, you are creating happiness. No one wakes up in the morning and says, "I think I will create misery today," but our unconscious thoughts *will* create our reality, whether misery or happiness. Now that you understand this principle, you can consciously create whatever you want.

Exercises
For Creating New Parenting Patterns

1. Make a list of some of your limiting beliefs.

2. Based on the limiting beliefs you listed above, change them to new empowering statements of belief.

3. Make a list of common negative thoughts you have and statements you often make, and change them to positive ones.

4. Take one of your new empowering beliefs, post it somewhere you will be sure to see every day, and repeat it often.

5. Help your child change one limiting belief to an empowering belief.

6. Tell your child the story of Morris Goodman, the miracle man, and then listen to what they have to say about it.

Is one right and the other wrong?
Two people can experience the same event and
each have a completely different experience.

CHAPTER 12
Perception

"It was the best of times, it was the worst of times." (Charles Dickens) Two people can experience the same event and each have a completely different experience. To one it can be a pleasant experience or of no significance at all. To the other it can be unpleasant or even traumatic. This does not mean that one view is right and the other wrong. It means the event is viewed from two different perspectives. This is why the same childhood experience is remembered differently by you than it is by your siblings or parents. *We see everything through the eyes of our own experience.*

When my children were young, we were all outside gardening and playing when a man came walking down the street and asked to use our phone. I was caught off guard and felt somewhat vulnerable with my small children. Out of fear and without much thought, I told him we did not have a phone and suggested he try a neighbor. My six year old was appalled that I had not told the truth. From my perspective, I was protecting my children, and I felt it was dangerous to let him in my house. (This was before the days of cordless or cell phones.) From my young child's perspective,

I told a lie. Who was right? Who had the correct perception? We both looked at the situation from our own experience.

"You never really understand a person until you consider things from his point of view." (Harper Lee, *To Kill a Mockingbird*) As adults, my daughter and I can now talk of this experience and understand why we both responded in different ways, not judging each other but just seeing from each other's perspective.

Our perceptions become our reality, and the more people who agree with them, the more we believe them to be true! We are influenced more by what we *think* is so than by what is *actually* so.

Look at the figure below. How many squares do you see?

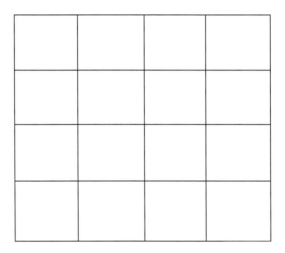

There is a total of 30. However, if you only see 16, 17, 21, or 25 then that is true also. Remember, the question is "How many squares do *you see?*" If you only see 16, then you only see 16. You are not wrong. It is just all that you see. And there *are* 16 squares.

Music is something we all have a perception about. When I hear a Bob Marley song, it reminds me of being on a bus in Belize. It was a wonderful experience of traveling with the local people on the rut-filled dirt roads as Bob Marley sang on the bus radio. Whenever I hear his music, it immediately makes me feel happy, like I was in Belize. Someone else may have a totally different reaction to the same song because of a different experience.

"We don't see things as they are. We see them as *we are*." (Anais Nin) It is as though we see things through colored glass. Our life's experiences color what we see. We have conflict because our experiences are different from each other. When we understand this we can step back and try to see the experience from another point of view.

I have worked with couples who have relationship issues, and I work with each one individually. I am always amazed at how they can each tell me about the same event, and I wonder if they are married to each other or someone else! They see the same thing though the eyes of their own life's experiences. Most differences can be resolved by intently listening to each other and remembering that your spouse has had a totally different life experience than you.

One man really got it right when he was listening to his wife complain that her brother was impossible to be around because he thought he was always right. She said her brother never gave her or anyone else a chance to speak freely or to have a different point of view. Her husband listened and then asked if she felt that her brother was very authoritative. She agreed. He then asked if she ever felt that way about her father. That was exactly how she felt about her father and now her brother. She gained insight into herself and her relationship with her brother because her husband had listened with intent to see things from her perspective. The results was not only harmony between husband and wife, but the wife's understanding of her feelings toward her brother. We assist each other when we listen with love and with intention to see through the eyes of one another.

To see a great example of how everyone in a family can have a totally different experience from the same event, watch the movie or read the book *My Sister's Keeper*. It is the story of a family whose young daughter has leukemia. You will see how each family member has their own experience and perceptions. When they all come to see things from the other's perspective, understanding and emotional healing occurs.

In our relationships with our children, they will benefit greatly when we listen with our hearts with intent to see their perspective. They have not had the experiences we have had, and *we* have not had the experiences *they* have had.

A child's perspective can be profoundly insightful. For example, as individuals and as groups of individuals, we all experience God in a different way. Even if you do not believe in God, you still have a perception based on your experiences. When we are willing to look at another's beliefs with respect and without trying to convince them that *we are right* and *they are wrong,* we can be more in harmony with each other. The following *perceptions* of God are humorous but are a wonderful example of how children view God based on their experience.

Dear God, Instead of letting people die and having to make new ones, why don't you just keep the ones you got now? Jane

Dear God, I went to this wedding and they kissed right in church. Is that OK? Neil

Dear God, Thank you for the baby brother but what I prayed for was a puppy. Joyce

Dear God, I think about you sometimes even when I'm not praying. Elliott

Dear God, I am American. What are you? Robert

Dear God, I bet it is very hard for you to love all of everybody in the whole world. There are only four people in our family and I can never do it. Nan

Dear God, If you watch in church on Sunday I will show you my new shoes. Mickey D.

Dear God, Please put another holiday between Christmas and Easter. There is nothing good in there now. Ginny

God, I would like to live 900 years like the guy in the bible. Love Chris

Dear God, If we come back as something, please don't let me be Jennifer Horton because I hate her. Denise

Dear God, If you give me genie lamp like Aladdin, I will give you anything you want except my money or my chess set. Raphael

We read Thos Edison made light, but in Sun School they said you did it, so I bet he stoled your idea. Sincerely, Donna

Dear God, Please send Dennis Clark to a different camp this year. Peter

Dear God, Maybe Cain and Abel would not kill each so much if they had their own rooms. It works with my brother. Larry

Dear God, If you let the dinosaur not extinct we would not have a country. You did the right thing. Jonathan

Dear God, I think the stapler is one of your greatest invention. Ruth N

Dear God, In bible times did they really talk that fancy? Jennifer

Doors

Once we understand the principle of perception and begin to use it in our lives, we will begin to see the endless ways of looking at things. Even when events are beyond our control, we can look at them in a different way, from a different perspective.

It has been said, "When one door closes another one opens." However, we must look for the open door and then step through it. When something happens in our lives and we can no longer live life the way we did, we can look at it as a closed door, stopping us from doing a certain thing, or we can look around us and find new doors. No matter how pained or devastated we feel as a door is closed, there are always new doors to new possibilities.

Winston Churchill said, "The pessimist sees difficulty in every opportunity. The optimist sees the opportunity in every difficulty." It is all in how you choose to see it.

Exercises
For Creating New Parenting Patterns

1. The next time you have a conflict with your child, stop and listen with your heart. See it from their perspective. Journal your experience.

2. Find a topic or project to discuss with your child. Ask them their opinion or ideas, and *really* listen and consider their point of view. If you find yourself thinking about what you are going to say next or how they are wrong or how the idea will not work, stop yourself and return to listening intently with your heart. Journal your experience.

3. What is something that happened in your life that you see as a door closing? List all the good things or blessings that you can think of from this event.

There is power in choice.
Give your child the right to choose and to be accountable.

CHAPTER 13
Choice & Accountability

Choose vs. Decide

We always have a choice. The problem is that many of us *decide* instead of *choose*. The word "decide" comes from the Latin root meaning "to cut off, to separate, to pass judgement, to bring to an end." Think of all the words ending in the suffix—cide: homicide, suicide, infanticide. Choice, on the other hand, implies that there are options from which to choose. If we do not like the results of our choices, we can choose again. There is power in choosing. Deciding cuts us off from other possibilities.

Many times we look at choices as right or wrong, good or bad. I prefer to use the words "working" or "not working." This way when I choose something that does not work for me, it frees me to choose again.

I worked with a young man who was addicted to drugs. He said he really messed up his life by making the wrong decision of becoming involved with drugs. He had so much guilt about it that he was stuck in his decision to abuse drugs and did so on a daily basis. Drug use brought a loss of freedom, loss of jobs, damaged relationships, and poor health. As he began to see that he made a choice that *did not work* for him, he could now look at other choices that might work better for him (choosing freedom, repairing relationships, holding down a job, and good health). When he looked at it as a choice instead of a decision, he began to let go of the guilt he felt that was keeping him stuck in his addictions.

This young man had grown up being told that using drugs was a "sin" and he needed to "repent." This resulted in much guilt. Let us look at the definitions of these words. The Greek definition of sin is "missing the mark." From this perspective, his choice to use drugs resulted in his missing the mark. For him the mark was freedom, good relationships, supporting himself with a job, and good health. Abuse of drugs resulted in his falling short of experiencing these things that he wanted. Repentance means "a change of mind, a fresh view about God, about oneself, and about the world." Now he can look at things again in a different way, change his mind, and choose again.

Guilt & Shame

Guilt and shame are negative emotions, along with fear, worry, and anger. It is not useful to hold on to any negative emotion. Guilt causes us to beat ourselves up, to feel that we are bad or evil, and to sink into depression and hopelessness. If something does not get us what we want, do not live in the powerlessness of guilt and shame. Choose an attitude of "That did not work. I do not like this result. I now choose something else."

Victim

Some of life's experiences leave us feeling like a victim: sickness, the loss or sickness of a loved one, financial loss, divorce, or not having the money or relationships we would like. However, we always have a choice. We can choose how to respond, and we can choose to see the blessing in it. We can choose to bless the situation and search out its meaning and the spiritual teaching. We can live a life of *choice* which is from conscious action, or a life of *chance* which is a life of unconscious reaction.

There are consequences to all of our choices. When we accept accountability for our choices, we can change our behavior so that it is in harmony with what brings us joy and happiness. You will feel empowered when you realize that you have the power to create whatever you want.

The following poem expresses how we can empower ourselves by realizing that we can wake up and choose a new path.

AUTOBIOGRAPHY IN FIVE SHORT CHAPTERS
By Portia Nelson

I
I walk down the street.
There is a deep hole in the sidewalk.
I fall in.
I am lost. I am hopeless.
It isn't my fault.
It takes forever to find a way out.

II
I walk down the same street.
There is a deep hole in the sidewalk.
I pretend I don't see it.
I fall in again.
I can't believe I am in the same place.
But, it isn't my fault.
It still takes a long time to get out.

III
I walk down the same street.
There is a deep hole in the sidewalk.
I see it there.
I still fall in. It's a habit.
My eyes are open.
I know where I am.
It is my fault. I get out immediately.
IV
I walk down the same street.
There is a deep hole in the sidewalk.
I walk around it.

V
I walk down another street.

Creating Consciously or Unconsciously?

It has been said that if you want to know what you really
want, look at what you have. Look at your health, your finances,
your relationships, your vocation. Whatever you have are the
consequences of your choices, whether conscious or unconscious.

Accountable people take responsibility for their successes as well as their failures. They look inward and not outward, and they do not blame. When we really get that we are the creators of our lives, we realize just how powerful we really are! When we make choices that are in alignment with our highest good, we get gratifying consequences. When we go against the grain of our divine nature, we experience pain.

Often people ask, "If I am the creator of my life, why in the world did I create this mess that I am in!?" It is a great question. No one would ever *consciously* create a bad relationship, an illness, the loss of a job, or the death of a loved one. No one wakes up in the morning and says, "Hmm. I think I'll create a turbulent marriage." *Unconsciously* we do it all the time.

Many years ago my husband and I were invited to participate as leaders in a youth retreat. It was a wonderful program but not something in which I wanted to participate. They needed couples instead of individuals to work with the youth, so my husband could not participate without me. He really wanted to do this, and I really did *not* want to do it. I did not want to disappoint him by refusing to be part of it. I just could not bring myself to be the wet blanket. Guess what happened? I got sick with chemical pneumonia and was hospitalized for ten days with a month-long recovery after my release. Now I was very sick so I did not *have* to do the retreat. I did not *have* to say no. I did not *have* to be the wet blanket. No one could be mad at me. Poor me! I was deathly ill! Would I have consciously given myself pneumonia so I could get out of this? Of course not. Would my subconscious create the illness? Yes. And it did.

Think back to a time in your life when you had an accident. What was going on in your life just before the accident? Almost everyone I have ever asked this to has remembered something emotional that was going on, and they immediately saw the connection, how they unconsciously created the accident.

Giving Kids a Choice

Children need to be taught the principle of choice and accountability early in their lives. Too often they are bombarded with *orders* from parents. The home should be a sanctuary and a place of learning but most of all, love, not a place of rigid orders to be followed to the tee. "Don't get in the street. Do your homework. Clean your room. Don't do drugs." Where is the choice? Who wants to live under a dictatorship? And what happens when mom and dad are not around to give orders?

Let us take just one of the above parental orders: "Don't do drugs." What if we approached it from the perspective of "Drugs are a choice."? Does that scare the heck out of you? Do you think that is just giving them permission to do drugs? Drugs *are* a choice. Ultimately they *will* choose. Give them your example of being drug free. Give them information about consequences (without scare tactics). Give them your overwhelming confidence in them. Give them the power of choice.

What if they choose drugs? There is always that chance. Of course you have to have boundaries. You have the right to choose a drug-free home. You have to protect yourself and your other children. You have the right to call 911 if you need protection. These are the consequences your child needs to experience if it comes to that. This sounds harsh and scary, but if there are no consequences to their behavior, and if you allow your boundaries to be trampled, you and your child will be stuck in dysfunction.

Let us take an easier example with a younger child. When my son was in grade school, it became a struggle to get him up and out of bed, ready for school, and on the school bus. The bus does not wait for sleepy children. If he missed the bus, either I had to drive him to school, or he missed school. He did not seem to mind my nagging, although it created much tension between us. I managed to get him on the bus, but I was stressed, drained of energy, and I was taking his responsibility away from him. One day after I saw the bus drive away, I asked myself, "What am I doing? I am not teaching him to be responsible. I am teaching him to be irresponsible. I am not allowing him his right to choose and be accountable."

I bought him a gift that day and presented it to him when he got home from school. It was an alarm clock. I taught him how to operate it. I apologized for treating him so disrespectfully by taking away his right to choose and be accountable for himself. From now on he could get himself up and ready for school. If he missed the bus, that would be okay, but I would not take him to school. He would have to miss school, and that was okay too, because I had plenty of work I could have him do at home. He would have to explain to the teacher why he missed school and did not have a written excuse from home. When they called, I would be truthful and explain that he chose to sleep in and miss school. I did not do this in an angry or punishing way. Just very matter of fact. He responded very well. I was no longer stressed. I was free again to enjoy my son instead of being a nagging, irritable parent. From that day forward he got himself up and to school. I never had the opportunity of letting him miss school, but I knew and he knew I would have made good on my word.

Exercises
For Creating New Parenting Patterns

1. Have a conversation with your child about "sin versus missing the mark" and "choice versus decide."

2. Tell them you would like to begin today to look at everything as "working" or "not working." What do they think about it?

3. List three things or areas of concern that you have told your child they should or should not do. Take one of them and write down all the positive and negative results that may occur. If appropriate talk to your child about it. Let them list the positive and negative results. They will probably come up with ones you have not thought of. Honor everything they say. After the list is complete, talk about it now being their choice.

As a man soweth, so shall he reap. (Holy Bible)

CHAPTER 14
Cause & Effect

Nothing happens by chance. Every action has a reaction or consequence. Some call this principal karma or "what goes around comes around." The Bible speaks of the law of the harvest, "As a man soweth, so shall he reap." Whatever shows up in your life is the result of your own creation, either conscious or unconscious. We are the cause *and* the effect.

This principal mandates that we take full responsibility for *everything* in our life. If we say we do not believe in the law of cause and effect, we are saying that "at any time, anything can happen, and we are powerless to influence what happens to us." When something "happens" we have two choices:

- We can be *aware* of what we are creating in our life, both positive and negative.
- Or we can *avoid* looking at how we are causing the effects in our life, crying, "It is not my fault!"

Spiritual -> Mental -> Emotional -> Physical

How do we create? We get it upside down sometimes. Our most powerful body is our spiritual body. It contains the power that creates all things. It is our life force. Our mental body is the part of us that makes the choice. The emotional body directs or moves the energy (E-motion or energy in motion). Our creation shows up in the physical body. It is obedient to the spiritual, mental, and emotional bodies.

Creating this way is no more secure or lasting than trying to balnce a pyramid on its tip.

The **Spiritual** is the source of all power and is the creative force or life force. The **Mental** makes the choice and directs the energy. How you feel **(Emotional)** will determine the form it will manifest. Then the **Physical** is obedient to what was started in the spiritual.

Creating from the Spiritual
is the surest way for lasting change.

I always ask my clients what their intention is at the beginning of each session. In other words, "What do you want?" They may say, "I do not want to be depressed anymore," or "I do not want to be an addict," or "I do not want to fight with my wife," or "I do not want to be overweight." Then I might ask, "What would you like instead of depression (or addiction, fighting, overweight)? What would your life *look* like if you were addiction-free? What would it look like to not be depressed? What would your relationship look like if you did not fight? What would your life look like if you maintained a normal weight?" Then I ask, "How would that *feel* to be free of addiction, depression, fighting, or overweight?"

I once worked with a woman who had such a hard time knowing what she wanted that we spent half of the first session figuring out exactly what she wanted. She really had never considered anything other than the depression she was experiencing. It was a breakthrough for her when she was able to realize what she wanted and to start creating that instead of continuing to create more of what she did not want. When she came in for the second session, she proudly announced, "I know what I want!"

Creating from the spiritual is choosing what you want and visualizing it. You move to the mental, then to the emotional, and finally it just shows up in the physical. Everything we want to create must be done in this order to experience lasting change.

Spend some time answering these questions about how you really want your life to be:

1. What do I want?
2. What would my life *look* like? (visualize)

3. How would that *feel*? (really feel how it would feel)
4. What is the first step to take for this to show up in the physical?

Here is an exercise you and your child can do to help you see how you have created what you have now and to create what you would rather have. Examples are given.

1. Write three thoughts you have on a regular basis.
2. What are these thoughts creating in your life?
3. Change any unwanted thoughts to new thoughts that will support what you would rather have.

1. Thought	2. What this creates in my life	3. New thought
No one likes me.	I do not have any friends	I like myself just the way I am. I am friendly to everyone I meet.
I am not attractive.	I do not take care of myself, eat right, or exercise. I do not even fix myself up when I go out.	I am loving myself, and I am doing healthy things for my body.
I am a poor athlete. I am just a couch potato.	I never try out for the team. I watch a lot of TV.	I am having fun playing sports. I feel good when I'm physically active.

Remember that there is no power in being a victim. Taking full responsibility for everything in our life gives us power to create whatever we want. It is our choice. WE ARE THE CREATOR OF OUR LIFE.

Exercises
For Creating New Parenting Patterns

1. Journal the questions on page 157 about how you want your life to be. Have your child do this exercise.

2. Journal the questions about changing your thoughts from page 158. Have your child do this exercise also.

Gratitude brings abundance.

CHAPTER 15
Abundance & Gratitude

O ne of the luxuries I enjoy is spending one-on-one time with my grandchildren. My three-year-old grandson was having his turn one day. We were not doing anything big, just hanging out. As we were putting together some lunch for ourselves, he casually said, "I am happy to be at your house today, Meemee." A simple heartfelt thank you was all it was. Unplanned by him, I am sure, and said so casually it could have gone unnoticed by me, but it was so sweet, so sincere. I felt his gratitude and wanted to shower him with the abundance of my love.

This is what the gift of gratitude creates: abundance, an abundance of all good things. It is so simple: *gratitude creates abundance*. The more thankful you are, the more abundance you create.

Before the beginning of a Life Skills class, I scattered a small paper cup full of pennies around the classroom: on the floor, the chairs, tables. I watched as everyone came in. Some noticed the pennies and just left them there. Others did not even notice. Others picked a chair to sit in that did not have any pennies on it. No one picked up the pennies. When everyone was settled in and the class began, I asked why no one picked up any pennies. Comments varied.

- "I didn't notice."
- "They were only pennies. Can't buy anything with just a few pennies."
- "I didn't think they were for me."

The analogy of this demonstration is that we often do not notice the abundance all around us. We do not think the good things out there are for us; they are for someone else. Little things are not worthy of appreciation.

Good things are all around us. If we do not notice them, they go unused by us, and they go away. We miss the blessing right in front of us. Little things are sometimes the most wonderful blessings to our lives. It can be what makes life sweet.

If you notice what you have, you get more of it. If you notice what you do *not* have, you get more of what you do not have. The way to get more of anything is to be thankful for what you do have. The pilgrims dug seven graves for every hut they built, but they still created a day of thanks which began our Thanksgiving.

One thing that feels good is having someone express a heartfelt thank you, as my little grandson did. It often only need be someone looking you in the eyes and saying "thank you" and knowing they really mean it. The thing that feels at least equally good is feeling and expressing gratitude to someone. It has been said that giving and receiving are the same. This seems to me to be the case with giving and receiving gratitude.

Here are some ideas to help yourself and your children to have an attitude of gratitude. Remember, focusing on the things for which you are grateful attracts health, wealth, and happiness.

- If something in your body is not healthy or working properly, bring your attention to the areas of your body for which you can be grateful. Example: A child with a disability of very poor eyesight could realize and be thankful for how keen his hearing is.
- If your car is old and the paint is peeling and you cannot afford a new one, find something about the old car you appreciate. Example: This old car is still dependable and gets me where I need to go, and it gets great gas milage.
- If your relationship with your teenage son is not what you would like it to be and he is trying your patience, find something good in the relationship for which to be thankful. Example: You are so kind to your little sister.

Gratitude brings abundance. It keeps us focused on the positive. The law of attraction means that whatever you focus on, you get more of. Like attracts like.

Looking for the Blessing

Often when unpleasant situations or even tragedies show up in our lives, we only see the bad. I have developed a habit of always looking for the blessing in every situation. It is always there. Sometimes it is not immediately seen, but it is always there. Because the blessing is always there, we can be grateful for *everything* in our life.

Most of all, be grateful for your child. Tell him every day something positive you see in him or her. Make it a habit. Let it become who you are—a grateful, always-looking-for-the-good, cheerful parent. Your child will mirror that back to you—a grateful, always-looking-for-the-good, cheerful child.

Exercises
For Creating New Parenting Patterns

1. Write down three things in your life that you see as negative (health issues, relationships, financial worries). Now shift your focus to something for which you can be grateful (see examples on page 162).

2. If appropriate, help your child do exercise 1.

3. Make a list of all the positive things you see in your child and all the things you appreciate about him or her.

4. Set aside one whole day for saying only positive things to your child. Journal your experience.

Health is a choice.
Choose to become healthy.

CHAPTER 16
Health & Healing

I believe that health is a choice, either conscious or unconscious. For the most part our society has fallen into the victim mentality when it comes to our health. We expect someone else to be responsible for our health. But when we realize the power we have to create even physical health, we can enjoy the freedom of a healthy, vibrant body. Either we create health or or we create dis-ease.

Spiritual. When we understand how to create (see chapter 14 Cause & Effect), we begin with the spiritual. Since the spirit is perfect and always healthy and powerful, we want to tap into this spiritual energy to create health.

Mental. Science now tells us that illness originates in the mind before it shows up in the body. And our limiting beliefs create our reality. Have you ever heard of a doctor telling a patient they have only six months (or another specific time) to live? Is the doctor so smart that he can predict when a person will die, or has he just helped his patient to create a limiting belief that he will die at the end of six months? If you believe it, you will create it.

Quantum physics tells us that every atom is more that 99.9999 percent empty space. The subatomic particles that move at lightning speed through this space are bundles of vibrating energy that carry information. This implies that with our thoughts we can govern what that information is. Could this be how our thoughts and beliefs create our reality? Is this how the mind directs the body? If so, then let us get busy with positive thoughts, affirmations, prayers, meditations, and visualizations.

Emotional. We can do many things for the physical body to help it heal. Some of these are listed in the next paragraph. But if we do not address the emotional cause, the dis-ease or illness will remain, or if the illness does leave, it will return, either the same one or a new one. Refer back to chapter 5 for more on emotions. It is the emotion that carries the creative thoughts of good health (or illness) into the physical body.

Physical. Here is a list of things for you and your child to do for the physical body. These will be easier and often happen quite naturally when we have created beginning with the spiritual, then the mental, and the emotional.

- Regular exercise
- Eat healthy food. Eliminate or minimize junk and anything harmful to the body.
- Supplements
- Clean, filtered water
- Adequate sleep

Be happy. Being healthy has been said to make us happy, but the truth is, it is the other way around. *Happiness creates health.* Here are some things that have shown to slow aging and create health:

- Prayer/meditation (getting your energy form your source/God)
- Satisfying long-term relationships
- Being able to create (workplace, school)
- Feelings of personal happiness
- Ability to laugh easily
- A satisfactory sex life [adults only:)]
- Ability to make and keep good friends
- Regular daily work routine
- At least one week's vacation every year
- Feeling in control of your personal life
- Enjoyable leisure time
- Satisfying hobbies
- Ability to express feelings easily
- Being optimistic about the future
- Feeling financially secure, living within your means

Be happy and love yourself. When you love yourself and your body, you will find that eating, exercise, and other things that are good for you come more naturally. Choose to become healthy. You are the creator of your life. You are not a victim. You are a powerful creator.

Exercises
For Creating New Parenting Patterns

1. Look at the list of things that have shown to slow aging and create health (page 168), and write down the ones at which you do really well. Congratulate yourself and celebrate your happiness.

2. From the same list, write down three things that need improvement. Pick one of these and journal the steps you plan to take to improve. Journal your success.

3. With your chid, discuss the areas under PHYSICAL and both of you list the things you do really well. Then list the things at which you could improve. Pick one area and work on it for one week.

Relax and watch your child grow and
bloom at his or her own pace.

CHAPTER 17
Harmony & Rhythm

Think about the rhythm in nature: the natural flow of the seasons, the rising and setting of the sun, the rise and fall of the ocean tide, and even the birds flying south every winter. We have our own rhythm and flow in our lives. We must honor this rhythm in our lives and in nature.

The Butterfly

A man found the cocoon of a butterfly. One day a small opening appeared. He sat and watched the butterfly for several hours as it struggled to force its body through that little hole. Then it seemed to stop making any progress. It appeared that it had gotten as far as it could, and could go no further.

Then the man decided to help the butterfly, so he took a pair of scissors and snipped off the remaining bit of the cocoon. The butterfly then emerged easily, but it had a swollen body and small, shriveled wings. The man continued to watch the butterfly because he expected that, at any moment, the wings would enlarge and expand to be able to support the body, which would contract in time.

Neither happened! In fact, the butterfly spent the rest of its life crawling around with a swollen body and shriveled wings. It was never able to fly.

Are we in a hurry for our child to do things he or she is not ready to do? I remember how impatient I was to have my children out of diapers. I put them in "big girl" and "big boy" underwear before they were ready, foolishly thinking that it would hasten the day that they were toilet trained. But nature took its time, and they passed through this stage when *they* were ready. We would have all been less stressed if I had just let my little butterflies emerge when they were ready, instead of trying to hurry up the process.

Many parents push their kids into a school environment too soon, dating relationships too soon, many things too soon. We somehow think that if we can get our child to talk or walk early that they will be better off. My child who walked at thirteen months walks just as well today as his sibling who took his first step at eight and a half months. They both walked when they were ready. I, on the other hand, did not walk until I was eighteen months old! Yes, I have always been a late bloomer, but I bloomed at my own pace, and I am doing just fine now, thank you.

Relax and watch your child grow and bloom at his or her own pace. Be patient with them and with yourself. Everything takes time. Are you trying to become healthy? It takes time. Just stay with it and be patient. As we are dealing with winter and waiting for things to get better, know that things will get better and spring always comes. The trouble with many of us is that we give up too early. The tide will always turn.

Doing anything takes time and must be done in the proper order. Try putting your socks on over your shoes and walk. Yes, you can walk that way, but it is not very comfortable. If you go very far, well, it just works better, does it not, to put the socks on first and then the shoes?

Balance

Be a balance of physical, emotional, mental, and spiritual. If we focus too much on spirituality, we are out of balance and probably cannot make a living. If we focus too much on the intellectual, we can not enjoy the sunset. Listen to your body. When the body is in balance, it sends out signals of comfort. When it is out of balance, it sends out signals of discomfort.

Pay attention to your internal rhythm. If you are always charging ahead and pushing yourself or your child, shift down to your natural rhythm. If you are hanging back and procrastinating, listen for the divine in you spurring you to take that step. There are times for bold and daring actions.

Help your child to create a balanced life. Help them to enjoy their life. Too much or too little school work, sports, play, or free time all create imbalance. Our homes get out of balance too. Notice when your home life is sending signals of discomfort, letting you know things are out of balance. Imbalance creates unhappiness in our homes. Family will either foster or hamper our child's development. Be in harmony. Be balanced. Be happy.

Exercises
For Creating New Parenting Patterns

1. List ways you may be pushing your child into things for which they are not ready. Journal ways you can allow them to bloom at their own pace.

2. Write the words *physical, emotional, mental,* and *spiritual.* List some of the things that you do in each of these areas. Notice where you are out of balance. Journal your plans to bring more balance to your life.

3. Ask your child what ways his or her life is out of balance? Ask them how you can help them to bring more balance to their lives.

Section IV
THE FUTURE

". . . . she just fell in love with me."

CHAPTER 18
Another Chance

During the early days of parenting my children, I longed for enough free time to take a leisurely bath. Actually it did not have to be leisurely. If I could just be alone in the bathroom long enough to take a normal bath without anyone knocking on the door insisting that they could not wait another second, I would have been happy. As they entered the teenage years, I sometimes wished for those early days back. When they began to leave home and I would look at their childhood pictures, I would long for the children who were now gone.

In the New Testament the apostle Paul expressed to the Philippines, ". . . for I have learned, in whatsoever state I am, therewith to be content." (Philippines 4:11) I too have learned (finally) to be content or present with where I am in life. If your child is a baby, be present and enjoy the sweetness of this wonderful stage. If he is a four-year-old boy who loves dirt and bugs, delight in his grimy little hands as he gives you his treasured latest find. If your child is now a teen, appreciate the independence she displays when she lets you know she looks at things differently from you.

Adult Children

If your child is grown, honor the magnificent adult this child has become, and create a new kind of relationship. I was talking to a friend recently and asked how her adult son was doing. He had gone through some very rough times in the past. She told me that although he had chosen a path much different from hers, that he was doing very well. She had recently visited with him, and they had a very good conversation. She made the following comment, "Even though he has chosen a life different from mine, he is experiencing peace in his life. I stand in awe at the man my child has become." This is what we want for our children and ourselves. Have confidence in them and allow them to live their lives the way they see fit. Allow yourself to stand in awe of your child.

I truly enjoy my children now that they are adults. I have come to accept their choices for their lives. Yes, it is sometimes painful to see them experience the results of those choices, but I know that even when they experience pain or dysfunction, they are creating what they need to learn life's lessons. It is their life to live, their lessons to learn. They need no judgement from me.

Now that my children are adults, I try not to give advice. If they ask my opinion about something with which they are struggling, my intention is to voice my opinion only when there is a feeling from spirit. I may give them suggestions when they ask, but I always end with saying, "You choose what is best for you. I have total confidence that whatever you choose will be the best thing for you." I really mean it when I tell them that. They are the only ones who can know the best course for their own lives. It is very freeing also not to be responsible for their lives. They are doing just fine without me thinking they are not competent enough to make their own choices.

All of us, at some time in our lives, will go through difficult situations in which we feel the need for the help of another soul. Not someone to take over and do it for us because we are inadequate, but just someone to *stand with us*. Someone to say, "I am so sorry you are going through this, but I am proud to stand with you while you go through it." This is what a real friend or parent can do for an adult child. Do not render them helpless and deficient. Assist by just standing with them as an equal without judging or taking over. Standing with them is often all that is needed.

As a parent of an adult child, you are also now free to pursue your own interests. Let go and live your life. What is next for you? One day I was shopping with my two daughters, and we saw a bus full of older women on an excursion. I said to my daughters, "You see that bus? You will never see me on that bus." When my children were young, I did not know exactly what I would do when that phase of my life was over, but I knew I would not be content with touring with a bus full of seniors or playing bingo.

Many parents, especially mothers, feel lost or empty when their children grow up and leave home. Some call it the empty nest phase. If you fall for the ego's deception (refer back to chapter 10) that you are what you do, then when you no longer have children in your care, you will ask yourself, "Who am I now?" However, if you realize that parent is just a role, but not who you are, then you are free to pursue whatever brings you joy and satisfaction. There are unlimited possibilities.

Grandchildren

No matter where we are on our parenting journey, we can awaken each day and choose a new way to parent and a new way to be.

If you have grandchildren, they give you the perfect opportunity to *be* different. I overheard a young mother say, "My little girl can do no wrong in her grandparents' eyes. When I was a child my mother would have never allowed me to turn the light switch on and off for very long without her scolding me. However, when I scold my daughter for doing that, my mother says, 'Oh, just let her be. It is not hurting a thing.'" I believe this grandmother realized that the fascination with being able to turn a light on and off was just not worth a scolding.

As a child growing up, our house was across the street from my mother's parents. I loved being able to visit my grandparents anytime I wanted. I always felt welcomed. If Grandma had a little bit of cornbread left over, it was mine for the asking. If I wanted to play checkers, Grandpa was glad to take me in a game and show me all the tricks. I thought he was the smartest man around. I treasure the stories of their life that I loved to hear while sitting with them on their big front porch. One of my most vivid memories was seeing them in their declining years holding hands and just looking at each other. I thought how wonderful it must be for a woman to still be so esteemed and loved by the man of her dreams even when she was saggy and wrinkled from age. Love was lived in my grandparents' home.

Grandparents seem to have learned how to just let kids *be*. They seem to have learned how to just *love*. In most cases children love to go to their grandparents' home, maybe more than anywhere else. And why not? Would you not look forward to walking into someone's home whose face lights up when they see you? Would you not love it if they hug you and treat you better than royalty, and you knew that in their kitchen were those special foods tucked away that they know you like? Would you not feel loved if they had a drawer with some of your clothes, so you can change into clean, dry clothes whenever you need? Would you not love to see your artwork displayed on their refrigerator? Do you not want to go somewhere where you are esteemed and where you feel loved just the way you are?

A grandparent, maybe like no one else, can assist a child in feeling unconditionally loved and accepted. Grandparents do not usually have to worry with all the day-to-day things of parenting. The focus can be on the simpleness of love, joy, fun, happiness, and just BEing.

Grandma Hazel

Grandma Hazel was just shy of her one-hundredth birthday when she said goodbye to her family, became sick for a short period of time, and passed away. I did not know her personally but knew of her because she was the great-grandmother to my grandchildren. From all accounts she lived a rich, full life and was loved by everyone who knew her. She was quite adventuresome going white water rafting in her nineties and entertaining everyone with her humorous stories.

My grandchildren only got to be around her at yearly family reunions, but she made a lasting impression in the limited time she was with them. My seven-year-old granddaughter had this to say when asked about the death of Grandma Hazel. "I didn't know Grandma Hazel for many years, but the first time she met me, she just *fell in love with me*." What a gift this woman gave, to cause a child to feel so loved that she would be remembered in this way.

I have always said that I plan on living healthily until I am a hundred years old. Grandma Hazel has taught me that it is not important how long I live or what I do while I am here, but rather how much I love and how much I cause others to *feel* loved. Love really is all there is.

Exercises
For Creating New Parenting Patterns

1. Where are you in your parenting journey? Make a list of the things you enjoy about it.

2. Make another list of the things you would like to add to that list to make it better.

3. If you have thoughts of guilt about how you could have been a better parent, forgive yourself. Remind yourself that you are choosing something different now. Journal your thoughts.

4. Write down ways you are doing things differently now.

5. Pick one new way you can parent differently now.

May we all awaken to the glorious truth of who we are.

CHAPTER 19
A Bright Future

*C*reating *your life consciously and from a place of love is the most important thing you can do to assist your child. I hope you are well on your way to becoming more confident and living a life of happiness and joy for yourself. Letting go of your fears and practicing the principles of conscious living will awaken you to new possibilities for creating an uncommon life for you and your child. You cannot take your child where you have not been. When you heal yourself of your fears and false perceptions, only then can you help your child in his journey to become a happy, confident human being.*

There is much fear and worry about the future of our planet. Global warming, climate changes, pollution, poverty, crime, war: all of these things are the reality of our planet. We hear the prophecies from Christian prophets and others who predict an "end of the world after times of much tribulation." This is not a pretty picture. Knowing the power of visualization, I wonder if our joint visual of a turbulent and destroyed earth is helping to create the very thing we fear. Are we creating the earth's devastating end with our joint belief?

I do not mean to discredit spiritual prophets who through the ages have warned us of how it could be, but is that what it is—just what it *could* be? I believe that free will is always honored and that we are in control of our own destiny. I believe that if we change ourselves, we change the world. That is the way it is in our individual lives. If we are abusing our physical body by overeating, under exercising, and other things that cause our bodies to become unhealthy, we will reap what we sow. One could then predict (or prophesy) that we will become sick, overweight, and unhealthy, but we can choose again. We can clean up our act and choose to take another path. We can change the prophecy that we will become unhealthy to the prophecy that we will become healthy. If we can change our own destiny, and we can, then does it not make sense that together we can change the destiny of the world?

Quantum physics would tell us that a devastating "end of the world" is only one possibility of what can happen to our planet. It also tells us that there are unlimited other possibilities we can choose. Let us *choose* something different. Let us *visualize* something different. Let us *create* something different. It starts with us. Are there things we need to do as communities and nations to change the outcome? Yes! But we must first change our hearts and ourselves. We must *be* the change.

Some would say we are running out of time, that there is so much that needs to change that it is an overwhelming task. I believe change can happen in an instant. I personally have seen people heal in an instant. I have seen others change their lives so fast that friends and families hardly recognized the "new" person. Think of an experience when an event happened or you had a realization that changed the course of your life in a huge way. It can happen like dominoes. One small thing moves, starting a chain of events that could quickly result in a major transformation of our world. There can also be things happening internally that no one knows about; then it will seem like miracles happening all at once.

Kindness

There is the old story of a conversation between the wind and the sun. The wind boasted of great strength. The sun suggested a contest to see who could get the man on the road to remove his coat. The wind was confident that he could force the man to remove his coat with his strong cold gust, but the harder the cold north wind blew, the tighter the man clutched his coat. The sun came out from behind the clouds and warmed the air. The man now unbuttoned his coat. The sun slowly grew brighter and brighter. Soon the man became so warm that he took off his coat. Let us approach ourselves, our children, and all of humanity as the sun did, slowly shining brighter and brighter and gently influencing those around us.

I heard of a recent survey of what men want most in a relationship. Their answer was surprising: *kindness*. Is that not what we all want? Just a little kindness? Who likes to be spoken to with harshness? Who wants the cold wind to force us to remove our coat? Do we not all prefer the gentle kindness of the warm sun? I believe all of us will respond to kindness, especially those of us who have been deeply hurt and have put up a protective shell around ourselves.

A young woman who came to me, on the verge of losing her family, broke down and cried when I treated her and her "errors of judgement" with kindness and understanding. She had experienced many people telling her she was throwing her life away and that she was making bad mistakes, but her healing began when she experienced kindness. The kindness is what got through the layers of negative events, beliefs, and behaviors of her life's experiences. These prevented her from feeling loved unconditionally and being able to see that she could create something different for herself and her children. Love, kindness, and gentleness opened the door for her healing.

Look past the behaviors of your child, and yourself, and the behaviors of all humanity to the truth of who we really are: spiritual beings having a human experience. When we see it from this perspective, it helps us put aside the harshness of judgements and act with kindness and love. When I experience seeing someone through eyes of love, it feels as if nothing else matters, and this feeling of love becomes my world and my reality. I believe this is how we can change the course of the planet. Seeing, feeling, and being love.

My Intention For You

My hope for the world is that we all live consciously and that we put our differences and judgements aside and just *love one another.* By doing this I believe that not only will we awaken, but the planet itself will have a spiritual awakening and wondrous things will happen. My intention for me is that I awaken fully to my divine purpose and do for you, my brothers and sisters on this planet, those things I came here to do. I desire to make a positive difference in your life. I know that writing this book is a part of my journey toward living this purpose. I hope that through this book, you have been touched, moved, and inspired in a way that will change your life, the lives of your children, and the lives of everyone whose path you cross.

At the beginning of this book I invited you to put aside all of your old notions and to consider some new ones as you read the book and now, as you finish the last page, consider both old and new notions and take those that work for you. Trust the Divine in you to know the truth of what works for you in being a more conscious human being, a more conscious parent, and in assisting your child to be happy and confident. May you, your child, and all the children on the planet live a conscious life. May you awaken to the glorious truth of who you are. Namaste`

Exercises
For Creating New Parenting Patterns

1. What would you like your future to be? Write down the things you see in your own bright future. Focus on these things. Journal your thoughts.

2. Practice kindness with your child and journal your experience.

3. Do you have any new notions about yourself and parenting as a result of reading this book?

APPENDAGES

Appendage A
A Letter to My Children

My dear children: Bethanne, LeAnne, Jonathan, Benjamin, and Samuel,

First my apologies. Please know that I always did the things in raising you that I thought were the best for you, doing the best I knew how at the time. Chapter one explains this, but I also know that the things you have experienced in your life, from me or others, are exactly what you needed for your own personal growth. It is my desire that you overcome and use to your advantage *everything* from your childhood as a means to become more conscious. It is my desire that you awaken and create a meaningful life of joy, whatever that means for you. I want for you, what you want for you.

You are my five master teachers. I have learned so much, and continue to learn so much from each of you.

In raising you, I learned a lot about myself. I learned that I had in myself more than I thought possible: that I could be on call 24/7 and not self destruct, that cleaning up your vomit or a bad diaper is truly a privilege and an expression of love, that a moment in the bathroom all by myself was a great way to relax, that watching you hit a home run or strike out were both equally gratifying, and that I have the capacity to love unconditionally no matter what.

I also learned valuable lessons from each of you individually, lessons that only you could teach. They are numerous, too numerous to list.

I learned how to let go with confidence and know that you know better than me what is best for you, and whether you learn life's lessons the hard way or the easy way, you will still learn and do what is best for you. I've heard you laugh and tell others, "Yea, Mom gave us all luggage when we graduated from high school. We know what that means!" I think it was my way of telling *myself* that it was time to let you do it on your own. Time to trust that you can make your life whatever you choose.

And you have done that. Your life is your own creation. I am honored to still be a part of it, but you are the Creator of your life. You are all doing a great job. Even when you create things that do not bring you happiness, I see you learning and evaluating, and figuring out how to do it differently so you can get what you would rather have.

I enjoy the relationships we have individually and as a family. I love the Sunday evening get-togethers and the conversations around the backyard campfires. I love that you enjoy playing foosball, going canoeing, boating, and the host of other activities we do together. I love that my daughters enjoy hanging out with me and the awakening conversations we have. I am honored that we are free and open to express almost anything. I love the men my boys have become. I enjoy seeing the love and kindness you show to each other, to your sisters, wives, and girlfriends, to me and dad, and to your nieces and nephew. I see the love and kindness you show to all.

I am honored to have walked with you as children and honored to know you now as adults. I am grateful to see you grow into the powerful spirit beings you are as you create your own lives. Thank you for traveling this earthly journey with me. Thank you for your patience with me as I awaken to my true self.

I love you,
Mom

APPENDAGE B
A Letter to my Parents

My dear Mom and Dad,

Words cannot express the gratitude I have for the two of you. You gave me life. You gave me love. You gave me the perfect environment for me to experience the things I needed for my own personal growth. It was perfect in every way. There is nothing you could have done differently to make my life any better.

I take full responsibility for every action I have taken in my own life. If I have excelled or if I have fallen short, I fully own my choices. I have said repeatedly in this book that we all do the best we know how at the time. That means that *you* did the very best you knew how to be good parents to me and my siblings. I know that to be true from the very core of my being. It also means that *I* did the very best I knew how to be a good daughter. If I did not respond in a way you would have liked, I ask for your forgiveness and understanding. I love you both and only did what I knew to do.

I have ached to eliminate your difficulties and longed to see you both experience more joy, but I honor you and your journey and know you are going through what you need for your own personal growth. I have only the utmost love, respect and appreciation for you both. You could not have been better parents. Thank you for the blessing to my life that you are.

I love you,
Camille

APPENDAGE C
Tapping

*T*his is my version of tapping that I use on myself and with my
clients. It is slightly different than what is taught by the Rapid Eye
Institute and the Emotional Freedom Technique (EFT).

This technique can be used for the following:

- Negative emotions
- Panic attacks
- Painful memories
- Pain
- Cravings
- Addictions

I.   Tap ridges of hands (1) together (like a karate chop; see
    diagram on following page) while saying three times,
    one of the following:

    - "Even though I feel (negative emotion), I totally and
      profoundly love and accept myself."

- "Even though I am having this experience of (name the traumatic experience), I totally and profoundly love and accept myself."
- "Even though I have this pain in my (wherever it is), I totally and profoundly love and accept myself."

II. Next tap on the following points (see diagram) while saying three or four times, "I release the fear of (say the emotion, craving, or pain)."

   2. Between eyebrows
   3. Sides of eyes
   4. Top of cheekbone under eyes
   5. Center of upper lip under nose
   6. Center of indentation in chin under lower lip
   7. Below collarbone
   8. Under arms four inches below armpits
   9. Top of each hand an inch below and between the knuckles of little finger and ring finger
   1. Ridges of hands (hit together

III. After you have reduced the intensity of the negative emotion as much as you think you can, tap on the same points making "I am" statements, such as
"I am happy. I am calm. I am love." You can also tap on the entire body saying these "I am" statements.

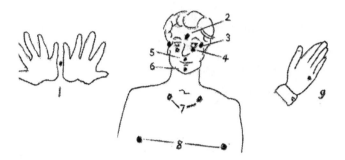

(Compliments of the Rapid Eye Institute)

The following may be helpful:

- Gauging the intensity of the emotion on a scale of one to ten (ten being very intense and one being very slight) will help you see how you are doing.
- The negative emotion many times will go away after one or two rounds of tapping.
- As long as the intensity is going down, continue to tap until it drops to a one or two.
- Sometimes a new emotion will come up. You may be tapping on a food craving, and the feeling of guilt may emerge. Just tap out guilt.
- If you are tapping out a headache and the intensity remains the same, ask yourself the following questions and just tap on the change.
- "Did it change in any way?"
- "Did it move?"
- "Did an emotion or negative thought come up?"

If you cannot clear your issue with the tapping, you may want to schedule a Rapid Eye session or find someone who is experienced with tapping or EFT.

BIBLIOGRAPHY
AND SUGGESTED READING

Byrne, Rhonda. *The Secret.* (Oregon: Beyond Words, 2006).

Chopra, Deepak, MD. *Perfect Weight.* (New York: Random House, 1994).

Dutra-St. John, Yvonne, and Rich Dutra-St. John. *Be The Hero You've Been Waiting For.* (Challenge Associates LLC, 2009).

Chamberlain, David. *The Mind of Your Newborn Baby.* (California: North Atlantic Books, 1998).

Emoto, Masaru. *The Hidden Messages in Water.* (Oregon: Beyond Words Publishing, Inc., 2004).

Hay, Louise L. *Heal Your Body.* (California: Hay House, Inc., 1984).

Hicks, Ester, and Jerry Hicks. *Ask and It Is Given.* (California: Hay House, Inc., 2004).

Hubbard, L. Ron. *Children, Scientology Handbook.* (New Era Pubns., 1997).

Jampolsky, Gerald G. MD. *Love is Letting Go of Fear.* (California: Ten speed Press, 2004).

Johnson, Marietta. *Organic Education, Teaching Without Failure.* (Alabama: Communication Graphics).

Johnson, Ranae. *Reclaim Your Light Through the Miracle of Rapid Eye Technology.* (Oregon; Ranae Johnson, 1996).

Kornfield, Jack. *A Path With Heart.* (New York: Bantam Books, 1993).

Lillard, Paula Polk. *Montessori Today.* (New York: Schocken Books Inc., 1996).

Namka, Lynne. *Good Bye Ouchies and Grouchies, Hello Happy Feelings.* (Arizona: Talk, Trust & Feel Therapeutics, 2005).

Neuman, M. Gary. *Helping Your Kids Cope with Divorce the Sandcastles Way.* (New York: Random House, 1998).

Seuss, Dr. *Horton Hears a Who.* (New York: Random House, Inc., 1954).

Tolle, Eckhart. *A New Earth, Awakening to Your Life's Purpose.* (New York: Plume, 2005).

Truman, Karol K. *Feelings, Buried Alive Never Die.* (Arizona: Olympus Distributing, 2003).

Tuttle, Carol. *Remembering Wholeness.* (Nebraska: iuniverse, 2000).

Waitzkin, Josh. *The Art of Learning.* (New York: Free Press, 2007).

Williamson, Marianne. *A Return to Love.* (New York: Harper Collins, 1996).

Zukav, Gary. *The Seat of the Soul.* (New York: Free Press, 2007).

Contact Information

- To order this book directly from the author or to find out other places to order you may go to www.ConsciousChildTheBook.com

- To contact the author you may email her at cbrowning46@bellsouth.net

- To find out more about Rapid Eye Technology or about the author you may go to www.rapideyetechnology.com

- To contact Bethanne Staton, the photographer, you may contact her at bethannestaton@aol.com

- You may also find Camille on facebook as Camille Browning, Rapid Eye Technician